D1116564

New Guinea
Tapeworms
and Jewish
Grandmothers

W · W · Norton & Company

NEW YORK · LONDON

New Guinea Tapeworms and Jewish Grandmothers

———————— • ————————

TALES OF PARASITES
AND PEOPLE

Robert S. Desowitz

Library of Congress Cataloging in Publication Data
Desowitz, Robert S.
  New Guinea tapeworms and Jewish grandmothers:
  tales of parasites and people.
  Includes index.
  1. Biology—Addresses, essays, lectures. I. Title.
QH311.D44 1981   574   81–1837
ISBN 0-393-01474-6   AACR2

W. W. Norton & Company, Inc. 500 Fifth Avenue, New York, N.Y. 10110
W. W. Norton & Company Ltd. 25 New Street Square, London EC4A 3NT

1 2 3 4 5 6 7 8 9 0

For
Carrolee

CONTENTS

Handwritten annotations:
- (ch.1) Intro to par. relation betw. man + monster
- (ch.2) Sweat for cooling; Exploitation of Daylight; Need for H₂O; relat. to parasites
- (ch.3) One Parasite ... Case Study
- (ch.4) Sickle cell, Malaria + Development
- (ch.5) G6PD, Fava, etc.
- (ch.6) Tsetse: Life Cycle, Effects, Treatment
- (ch.7) Black Flies and Onchocerciasis
- (ch.8) Schisto, Snails, etc.
- (ch.9) Benefits of Malaria?
- (ch.10) Parasitic Worms Cause and do not cause asthma
- (ch.11) Babeosis and Ticks
- (ch.12) Anisakiasis from raw fish / a marine worm
- (ch.13) Giardiasis world-wide
- (ch.14) Successful and Unsuccessful Pathogen control

New Guinea
Tapeworms
and Jewish
Grandmothers

1

PARASITES, PROGRESS,

AND THE PAST

Some time ago, while at London's Heathrow Airport on
the way to Burma, I had occasion to use what the
English genteelly refer to as the public convenience, and
there I was startled to find a government poster warn-
ing the traveler of malaria, symbolized by a Godzilla-
sized mosquito pouncing on a helpless world. Gazing at
it, I mused that when malaria takes pride of place over
venereal disease on urinal walls, the world's balance of
illness must have undergone a profound change. There
was a personal irony for me in this official concern. The
poster summoned a cascade of memories, recalling the
day twenty-seven years earlier when I had waited at
Heathrow for the flight that would take me to Africa
and to my first experience of the tropics and its diseases.

I had then just completed my studies at the London
School of Hygiene and Tropical Medicine. When the
prospect of ejection into a cold and jobless world had
begun to loom on my youthful horizon, my professor,
"the Colonel," had come to the rescue. The Colonel was

H. E. Shortt, a doyen among malariologists. My ultimate ambition was to tread softly in his giant footsteps. But this was not to be. Through the freemasonry that existed among former officers of the Indian Medical Service he arranged for my appointment to His majesty's Colonial Medical Research Service (despite the technical awkwardness of my American citizenship). I was thus posted to the newly created West African Institute for Trypanosomiasis Research in Nigeria, directed by another onetime Indian Medical Service colonel-malariologist, a man of rare wit and high charm, Hugh Mulligan. Why trypanosomes and not malaria? The Colonel was firm. "Desowitz, malaria is about to be totally eradicated, and you will never make a career, let alone a living, from it."

In the 1950s it did indeed appear that the ancient scourge of malaria was about to be sprayed into extinction. The World Health Organization's medical messiahs in Geneva, now armed with DDT and the potent, inexpensive antimalarial drug chloroquine, were leading this great crusade. The strategy was founded on mathematical calculations that had been made by English epidemiologist George Macdonald. These indicated that if DDT was assiduously applied for a certain number of years, the density of the anopheline-mosquito vectors* would fall so low that no transmission would take place. Eventually just about all human cases

*Certain disease-causing parasites are conveyed from an infected human or animal—the host—to another host by an invertebrate, such as the mosquito that transmits malaria. The transmitting organism is known as the vector. The life cycle of certain parasites, such as the malaria parasite, includes an obligatory phase in the vector, during which they undergo the transformation that leave them in the infective stage. In these cases, the vector is technically referred to as an intermediate host.

would become naturally "burnt out." The few strag-
glers—residual infections—could then be chemothera-
peutically eliminated. Thus, about ten years after the
first spritz of DDT, the malaria parasite would join the
dodo as an exterminated species. Unfortunately, the
mosquito and the malaria parasite, being neither epidemiologists nor mathematicians, didn't follow the
script. With dogged determination and in relatively
short order the mosquito became resistant to DDT and
other insecticides. For its part, the malaria parasite
became widely resistant to chloroquine and several
other antimalarial drugs. By the 1970s malaria was all
too alive and well. It was killing and debilitating with
unrestrained ferocity; there were at least a million
deaths a year from malaria in Africa, and 20 million to
200 million cases (no one knows the true figure)
annually in India.

This parlous state of affairs was brought into focus
for me when, a few days after my revelation in the men's
room, I arrived in Burma's capital, Rangoon, and visited the minister of health. In my role as (temporary)
Wise Man from the World Health Organization, I was
alleged to bear good tidings and sound advice. We
engaged in a high-anxiety conversation on the medical
sorrows of the country. Malaria is knocking them dead
in Burma. The minister estimated that in rural areas 75
percent of those seeking medical attention did so
because of malaria. With each passing year more and
more cases are resistant to treatment with the relatively
inexpensive antimalarial drug chloroquine, and the
newer, more effective drugs are beyond the pocketbook
of both government and people. The minister was
obviously preoccupied with malaria, but almost as an
afterthought, he turned the conversation to the other

problems that related to my consultantship in mosquito-transmitted infections. Dengue hemorrhagic fever from time to time sweeps through Rangoon, killing hundreds of children. Filariasis is always present in the large cities but may also be endemic elsewhere. No one is sure. Were there, I asked, problems with other, non-vector-borne, infectious diseases? Well, of course everyone had intestinal parasites, but they were too common to do anything about—a natural phenomenon. Water-borne bacterial intestinal infections also are taken for granted, although frequent outbreaks of cholera did give a dimension of urgency to that problem. "And thank you for coming to our assistance, Professor Desowitz. We look forward to reading your report." I walked out of the minister's air-conditioned sanctuary into the heat of the Rangoon day feeling as if I had been bludgeoned with a cudgel of microbes.

During the following weeks, as I traveled about the country and talked to villagers, physicians, and auxiliary health workers, the impact of infectious diseases and the dilemma of their control became all too apparent. The Burmese, after unshackling themselves from colonial rule, adopted a socialist political and economic structure tempered by the gentle Buddhist philosophy that deeply pervades their lives and thought. Burma is not one of the more affluent Asian nations. The country is economically hard pressed, but even so, the Burmese have mobilized their dedicated medical personnel, moved by the political-religious conviction that to "do right" requires bringing medical care to all the people, whether city dwellers or farmers in the smallest, remotest hamlet. Their health services have been largely decentralized; the physician, the barefoot doctor, the midwife—all the health workers of a village or, in the larger cities, of a township unit—come under the direct management of an elected health committee. This local control has made the medical personnel highly responsive to the health needs of the community they serve. It has also made each community aware of its own health problems. So when I discussed these issues over innumerable cups of tea it was with villagers who had given informed consent to their health program in the very broadest, most meaningful way. Almost invariably, when asked what they required in the way of medical supplies and services, they first emphasized an assured stock of antimalarial pills and worm medicines. (Occasionally a village elder assured me that an unripe banana will give you malaria every time.) They requested a safer water supply to halt their constantly recurring intestinal infections. They didn't ask for hospitals, or kidney-dialysis units, or even X-ray machines. They recognized the common infectious diseases as the main threat to their health and drain on their energies. The options open were not always easy. In some situations people had to make the hard choice between health and livelihood. In Arakan, bordering Bangladesh, I visited a town beset by malaria. Government malaria workers had identified the vector here as *Anopheles annularis,* a mosquito that was breeding prolifically in the shade of the vegetation in the many man-made ponds scattered throughout the town and its environs. Malaria control was an almost ridiculously simple matter of clearing away the vegetation. This was done in several demonstration ponds. The malaria-control people were happy; the village health committee was delighted; but the local population protested vehemently, and in spite of the success in the demonstration ponds the project had to be brought to a halt. It turned out that the vegetation was not a mean weed, but carefully nurtured water lettuce, a staple of the local diet and one of the townspeople's few marketable crops. The villagers, precariously balanced between grinding poverty and malaria-induced debility, had no recourse but to opt for the water lettuce.

Instances of increasing, uncontrolled (or uncontrollable) infectious disease, and the human tragedies that are left in its wake, are not peculiar to Burma. These vignettes can stand as object lessons of what is happening today throughout most of the tropical world. The names of the pathogens may change from region to region; the ecological-epidemiological elements that contribute to endemicity may change; but the undeniable picture is of an enormous tropical belt in which the ancient diseases are not only firmly entrenched but extending their dominion and intensifying.

That is the situation in the tropics. Despite hope and effort, we who work in tropical medicine accept the fact that these impoverished lands will be under the pall of disease for the foreseeable future. In contrast, those who live in affluent, industrialized societies are complacent, apparently protected against infectious diseases. That complacency is based on a delusion. Our containerized foods, gleaming toilets, and generally sanitized lives have not afforded complete protection. Amoebiasis and giardiasis (see chapter 13) occur in the American gut with chronic persistence and an occasional severe outbreak. In a kind of class warfare, the arthropod parasitic mite *Sarcoptes scabei,* the cause of scabies, has come to afflict people in the higher tax brackets. Pinworms, *Trichomonas vaginalis* (a cause of vaginitis in females and urethral disease in males), and *Toxoplasma gondii* (a protozoan parasite that can cause blindness and severe neurological disease in the newborn) infect citizens without regard to race, creed, or economic class. We seem defenseless against new variants of the influenza virus, and strains of gonorrhea bacteria have arisen that actually thrive on penicillin. Hospitals that had once controlled postsurgery infections through scrupulous cleanliness relaxed that aseptic vigilance when they adopted antibiotic prophylaxis. Now many bacteria have become antibiotic-resistant and some hospitals are breeding grounds of infection. To complicate matters, medical science has been bewildered by the appearance of infectious diseases, among them legionnaires' disease, Lassa fever, and babesiosis (see chapter 11), that are completely new to human experience.

Paradoxically, some forms of medical treatment may cause certain benign parasites to act as highly virulent pathogens. For example, a quiescent, asymptomatic infection of the protozoan *T. gondii* (which 30 percent of the population may carry) may become explosively lethal in a patient given steroids or other immunosuppressive drugs for the treatment of cancer or autoimmune disease or for the facilitation of an organ transplant. The infectious-disease problems of immunologically compromised patients are currently causing great concern to the medical profession.

We have become dependent upon the "quick fix" of chemotherapeutic magic bullets. There is no denying that these potent agents have saved countless lives and have freed us from the pervasive undercurrent of fear of these infectious diseases. My own childhood was in the decade preceding the discovery of the sulfa drugs, antibiotics, and polio vaccine. I still have the shards of dread when I recall my parents' anxiety that I might be stricken with polio, pneumonia, or meningitis. This was

no empty concern. From time to time one of my play-
mates would be taken ill with a feared infection and
there would be whispered talk that the unfortunate
child might die or become crippled or suffer brain damage. And for me there would be, at these times, a period
of quarantinelike overprotection. The discovery in the
1950s and 1960s of powerful antimicrobial drugs and
biological agents was instrumental in halting the slaughter of children and young adults (those most at risk) by
these infections. Of course it helps to live in an nation
and to belong to an affluent economic class.

Before the dawn of the drug era, sanitary measures,
such as draining swamps to prevent the breeding of the
malaria mosquito, were the chief means of controlling
many major infectious diseases. Sanitation was reason-
ably effective as long as the effort was sustained. But
sustaining it was hard work; it is certainly easier to
distribute pills than to drain a swamp. Unfortunately,
the pills too often have not fulfilled their promise. Some
pathogens, such as certain strains of the malaria parasite, have become drug-resistant. Some drugs have
turned out to be too toxic. Or, more simply, people have
just refused to take the allotted pills. Meanwhile, all too
often the sanitary measures have been neglected, and
the environment has begun to deteriorate, in the
hygienic sense, in many areas of both the developed and
the underdeveloped world. Indeed, the two central
themes of this book are (1) that man-made ecological-
environmental changes have been responsible for perpetuating and intensifying the majority of infectious
diseases, and (2) that ultimately effective control of these
infections will follow widespread use of the time-
honored, sensible approach of environmental sanitation.

American readers gasping in Los Angeles smog, sickened by toxic waste, or languishing in a city slum need no reminder of the impact of environmental deterioration on their health. Environmental decay in the Third World has had an even greater effect on the health of the people. In the name of progress great rain forests have been leveled, savanna grasslands overexploited, and rivers dammed; these ecological perturbations have, as will be described in succeeding chapters, led to the spread of such diseases as malaria, sleeping sickness, river blindness, and other infections. Tropical cities too have been touched with the taint of decay. The cities of the tropics have within the last two or three decades been subject to an explosive, uncontrolled growth, resulting in the creation of sprawling "instant slums." Sanitary facilities have not been expanded to accommodate this growth. In many of these cities the water-waste systems have become so hopelessly antiquated that sufficient capital will perhaps never be available to provide a water supply that permits the householder (or tourist) to turn on the tap and drink with impunity.

Ailing Burma, again, exemplifies this morbid turn of events. Its capital city, Rangoon, is a delightful, exotic place in which to recapture the past—particularly if you are over forty-five. When I went to a party there in 1979 the local *jeunesse dorée* were doing the twist. On the other hand, nostalgia has its limits. The sewage system was constructed in the 1890s, when the city's population was 200,000. The population is now about 2 million, but the sewage system is unchanged. The Ragoonite's toilet doesn't flush—no trouble . . . just knock a hole in the pipe and let it all flow out . . . into the streets. To the citizens of Rangoon, as to people throughout the fecalized tropics, formed feces are abnormal. The diarrheic norm is accepted, for, after all, one hardly realizes one is ill if one is never truly well. I once participated in a study in the abjectly poor region of northeastern Thailand to find organisms responsible for enteric infections that were highly endemic there. In almost all cases the fecal specimen sloshed around liquidly in the collection cup. The donor asked how long he or she had had diarrhea, would almost always reply, "What do you mean, diarrhea? My stool is always like this."

Those in the tropics whose health has been most affected by ecological alterations are the farmers of the forest and savanna. The infections involved have most often been the ones caused by vector-borne parasites,* because disturbances of tropical ecosystems frequently produce environmental conditions highly favorable for the proliferation of the vectors. Each vector—blackfly, snail, mosquito, or whatever—has its own life requirements. One species of mosquito, for example, breeds only in sunlit, well-oxygenated water; a second species breeds in small, shallow pools; another requires open water with suitable aquatic vegetation; and still another must have brackish water and will breed only near the sea. If alterations in the environment remove the needed conditions, the vector becomes biologically

---

*In the broadest sense, a parasite is an organism living in complete dependency in or on another living organism, the host. The host shields the parasite from the harsh outer world and supplies its food. The host is the parasite's restaurant; indeed, the term *parasite* is from a Greek word meaning "one who eats off the table of another." All living creatures are hosts to parasites, which range in size from the smallest virus, of sixty angstroms (an angstrom is one ten-billionth of a meter), to a tapeworm forty-five feet long. In the course of evolution all kinds of species, representing virtually every phylum of the plant and animal kingdoms, have adapted to a parasitic way of life. This book, however, is mostly about animal parasites—protozoa and worms (flat, round, and tape).

bankrupt. But ecological alterations may also create a habitat highly suitable for a vector; in that case it will flourish, and transmission of the infection it carries will increase. For example, chopping down the trees in an African rain forest exposes the small ground water to sunlight. These sunlit pools are ideal breeding habitats for the highly efficient vector of malaria, *Anopheles gambiae.*

For blood-sucking vectors, a particularly important epidemiological determinant is feeding behavior. A species of mosquito or tsetse fly may be as finicky in its food preferences as a strong-willed three-year-old child. Hence, a species of anopheline mosquito which is perfectly capable of transmitting malaria may in fact not do so, because it prefers to feed on domestic animals rather than humans.

Thus, while each vector has its behavioral limitations (and don't we all?) none is a genetic robot; each has some latitude in which to exercise choice if conditions so demand. If the water buffalo that constitutes the preferred source of blood is replaced by a tractor, the mosquito will divert to humans rather than attempt to make a meal of diesel oil. Diversion of this kind is of obvious importance in the dynamics of transmission; it has, in fact, occurred in numerous instances.

Sometimes the train of events and behavioral alterations that brings disease in epidemic proportions has a dominolike subtlety. Recently, there was a savage outbreak in northern Thailand of "tractor-induced" Japanese encephalitis, a virus infection transmitted by the mosquito *Culex tritaeniorhynchus,* which breeds in wet rice paddies. This virus proliferates in the pig to such an extent that virologists refer to the pig as an amplifying host; it cannot infect the water buffalo. The traditional practice in northern Thailand was to plow the rice paddies with water buffaloes and keep pigs for food and market. Since *C. tritaeniorhynchus* prefers steak to pork, the water buffaloes acted as a "blotter," limiting viral transmission. Then, heeding the call of progress, the farmers of the region replaced their buffaloes with tractors. As the buffalo population declined, the mosquitoes turned their attention to the pig and to man. Many pigs now became infected; the virus multiplied in the pigs; more and more mosquitoes became infected; and, in turn, so did more and more humans. Hundreds died, and many of these victims were children. Only when the rice fields were massively sprayed by airplane was the epidemic brought under control.

These deaths could have been prevented. The scientific knowledge needed to predict these events was available, as was the national and international expertise to convey it to the authorities. The failure to exploit that knowledge is outrageously tragic. In other situations the members of the biomedical community have not been so remiss; they are increasingly aware of the epidemiological consequences of the ecological alterations wrought by agricultural and water-impoundment projects. Unfortunately, however, more often than not we have neither the resources nor the techniques to stem these "man-made" illnesses.

What I consider the paramount outrage is that the people who will be affected are so rarely allowed to decide how they shall live. Villagers near the site of a proposed dam and the lake it will create are not informed that although their crops will increase, they and their children will undoubtedly contract schisto-somiasis and malaria once the lake has filled. They are not permitted to weigh the advantages and the risks of the scheme and then accept or reject it. The political and technological authorities who arrogate the decision making to themselves treat them with contempt, as expendable, ignorant peasants. And once the dam is built, the only ones to benefit from the cheap hydroelectric power are those living in the cities several hundred miles downstream. You can bet on it; the now sickened villagers do not get electric lights in their huts.

Viewing the tapestry of medical history, we naturally fix our attention on the contemporary scene. We are most concerned with the here and now, the afflictions that threaten us as individuals and as a community. However, when we step back and look at the whole tapestry we see a panorama of conflict between human and pathogen that has been continuous over the millennia. The tide of war ebbs and flows. Plagues and pestilences come and go. Malaria is halted, then recrudesces. Occasionally one combatant or the other wins a great victory. The battle is joined, and smallpox is eradicated. Another virus increases its virulence, and a human population is exterminated or so reduced in numbers that it will gradually disappear. The details of the tapestry are clear only for the period of recorded history, which represents just a scrap of time. During most of our residence on earth we have been hunter-gatherers. The shadowy past may go back half a million or a million years, perhaps even further. But only since the development of agriculture some ten thousand years ago has there been any recorded history.

The dry bones of our very early ancestors have provided disappointingly few clues to the kinds of diseases prevalent during the aeons of prehistory. Paleopathologists—scientists who retrospectively diagnose disease and infections from fossilized remains and mummies—

have found evidence that the Neanderthals suffered from arthritis (as did dinosaurs, they declare) and from frequent traumatic injury. Then, about ten thousand years ago, relatively late in the day and at a time when agricultural settlements were beginning to form, there occurred quite suddenly a veritable pandemic of a disease that caused anemia. Many bones from that era, particularly those unearthed from the Mediterranean littoral, show an abnormality, known as porotic hyperostosis, in which the marrow space is greatly expanded. Bone marrow, the tissue that manufactures red blood cells, increases in volume to compensate for the loss of these cells in anemia. Some paleopathologists attribute the widespread anemia of that time to the first appearance of *Plasmodium falciparum* malaria as a human infection. Others believe it was due to hookworm infestation, a common condition today in tropical and subtropical agricultural peoples. Still others believe it was due to malnutrition. The mystery has baffled paleopathologists for many years, and we shall probably never know the answer.

Except for those found in bones, the clues to the nature of Stone Age diseases are few. (Mummies are of no help since they are, relatively speaking, practically contemporary.) One of my colleagues conducted an intriguing search for the eggs of parasitic worms in the fossilized feces of pre-Columbian Central American Indians. He concluded that the only intestinal parasitic worm in the Americas before the coming of the Europeans (and their worms) was the pinworm, *Enterobius vermicularis*.

Although dead men tell few tales regarding prehistoric medical history, a few remnant groups of hunter-gatherers can serve us as living examples of the way we were. The hunter-gatherers of Asia, Africa, and tropical America share at least two characteristics: they live in small social groups that have only limited contact, and they are nomadic, with even those practicing rudimentary agriculture shifting from place to place. Because the bands are usually composed of no more than twenty-five to fifty individuals, the only communicable diseases that can be perpetuated within a group are those of indolent, long persistence and those of animal origin.* Hunter-gatherers live in harmonious intimacy with their habitat, not causing any ecological alterations that are of epidemiological consequence. Those who dwell in the tropical rain forests are not at great risk to malaria (there are few breeding sites for anopheline vectors in that ecosystem, providing it remains undisturbed) or, in Africa, to sleeping sickness (the ecosystem in this case is *so* favorable for the vector, the tsetse fly, that it is dispersed and there is little man–fly contact). They do not suffer from the common cold or from toothache. Their blood pressure is so low that it would make any urban hypertensive weep in envy. And yet, despite this robustness their lives are pitifully short; few survive beyond the age of forty. This is a paradox. The causes contributing to early death among the hunter-gatherers are not fully known. Certainly the hazards of nomadic life, and the ravages of the communicable diseases, such as tuberculosis, to which they are subject, must take their toll.

Nor do we have an accurate understanding of the regulatory factors that cause the population of hunter-

---

*In chapter 2 I discuss the concept that each communicable disease—i.e., each infection by a parasite, whether viral, bacterial, or animal— requires a minimum number of hosts, the "critical mass," if it is to be perpetuated in any particular group.

gatherers to remain limited veneration upon generation. The IUD and the Pill have not come to the
Babinga of Gabon, the Guyaki of Paraguay, or the
Punan of Kalimantan. In many tribes sexual taboos are
observed after the birth of an infant. A few tribal
groups practice infanticide to stem population increase.
Some groups employ abortion-inducing medicines
derived from the plants of their ecosystem. Sterility
caused by venereal disease, prevalent in some hunter-
gatherer groups, is still another factor that controls population growth. But whether these controls alone maintain the population steady state is debatable. As far as
can be determined, the communicable diseases that
account for the high mortality of the young among
primitive farmers and the rural poor (with as many as
40 percent dying before the age of two) do not seem to
afflict the young of hunter-gatherers.

Most hunter-gatherers are now turning to agriculture
and settling down, and their habitats are more and
more being subjected to irreversible, exploitive destruction. As for other tropical peoples, they too are experi-
encing population pressures, new infections arising
from outside contacts and alterations in their habitats,
and the physiological aberrations of civilization, notably
hypertension and anxiety.

Some aspects of this transition are not without a cast
of black humor. The renowned French ethnobotanist
Jacques Barrau tells a story of his experience with the
Ituri forest pygmies of the Congo. He was collecting
medicinal plants that they use, and while accompanying
them to their "drugstore" he came upon a forest clearing that was under cultivation. As Barrau tells it, the
sight made him breathless with excitement. He felt that
he was witnessing within the microcosm of that steam-

ing rain forest, the first transition of man from a life of hunting-gathering to incipient agriculture. But what would the first crop of these primitive people be? At this point in the story Barrau, a raconteur with a fine Gallic sense of timing, pauses. He moved closer and examined a plant. It was marijuana!

For Barrau, an anthropologist-botanist, this is a phenomenon of social change, an example of the corruptive impact of the world beyond the forest sanctuary. Desowitz, a medical ecologist, listens to the story, is amused, and has a different vision. Perhaps that is the difficulty. Each specialist has a different vision, limited by the blinkers of his or her expertise. I see this small perturbation of the tropical forest as having potential epidemiological consequences far beyond the modest physical change. The small clearing will undoubtedly produce a favorable habitat for the highly efficient mosquito vectors of malaria. I see the members of this hunter-gatherer group forsaking their unrestricted mobility as they become bound to their garden plots. And with this attachment to the soil the floodgate that has been a faithful barrier to water-associated infectious disease will open, ushering in lowered nutrition and the diseases of civilization. The undisturbed forest was protective of its human component. This was the ecology of Eden. Now the first bite has been taken in the apple of progress—and there is a worm within its core.

2

THE UNIFIED THEORY
OF PERSPIRATION, EVOLUTION,
AND INFECTION

A castle perched high in the Austrian Tyrol is an unlikely setting for the origin of what I will pompously—and half seriously— call "the unified theory of perspiration, evolution, and infection." It was in the Tyrol that a meeting organized by the Wenner-Gren Foundation for Anthropological Research was held, at the Burg Wartenstein castle, the Foundation's conference center. This week-long scholarly kaffeeklatsch brought together, in monastic but majestic isolation, a group of experts to attack the topic of human ecology in the tropical savannas. During that week the vast ecosystem that occupies a large part of the earth's tropical girdle was never far from our thoughts.

One evening Professor Joe Weiner and I were having a postprandial discussion on the requirements for physiological adaptation to the relatively arid conditions of the savanna. Joe is an enthusiastic maestro of many sciences—a physician, physiologist, and anthropologist (he was instrumental in blowing the whistle on the Piltdown forgery). "You know," Joe remarked, "what we really have been talking about all week is not grasses and trees, but water. In the savanna, human settlement, adaptations, and the ecological perturbations that affect us are all based on the water supply. Humans require a lot of water in the savanna. They sweat a lot. Come to that, only humans really sweat and only humans use sweat to control body temperature." That seemed like a strikingly seminal observation, and to pursue the matter further we uncorked another bottle of wine and reached for another piece of strudel; and in this way the peculiar perspiration hypothesis was conceived.

As I write, the theory still seems peculiar, although my physiologist colleagues assure me of its logic. It takes us back to that still-obscure fork in the road where hominid or early human walked, upright, down a different path from that taken by creatures that were to continue the primate line. Conventional commentary has selectively chosen certain characteristics as setting us apart from the beasts—the progressively enlarging forebrain and the cunningly designed opposable thumb, a thumb that facilitated manufacture of the tools conceived by that progressively enlarging forebrain. Ignored is another anatomical-physiological adaptation that was to make us unique: we began to sweat. And we have been sweating ever since—gloriously, copiously.

The skin of all mammals functions as a radiator. There is a massive network of small veins and arteries, and when blood flows through this system, heat is given up in the form of radiant energy. This process keeps us cool—but only to a degree. At about 88°F (31°C)— exactly when depends on the level of heat adaptation of the individual—the radiant-energy method of heat disposal does not suffice and in humans a second air-conditioning unit switches on; the sweat glands secrete their salty, watery fluid. Evaporation of sweat over the entire body surface is then the main thermoregulatory mechanism. Under extreme conditions of heat and work, as much as three gallons of sweat may be produced in twenty-four hours.

Two kinds of secretory glands (in addition to the sebaceous glands associated with the hair follicles) are present in the skin of all mammals—the apocrine glands and the eccrine glands. The apocrine glands secrete a milky fluid, which gives the lather to horses and the body odor to humans. They are distributed throughout the skin in animals, but in humans are limited to the armpits and the areas around the nipples, the belly button, and the genitalia. Apocrine glands do not respond to thermal stimuli; their secretions do not help to control temperature. The heat of emotion rather than the heat of the day turns on apocrine activity.

The eccrine glands are the true sweat glands, the glands of perspiration, a secretion which is 99 percent water and 1 percent organic and inorganic salts. Animals have few eccrine glands, and these are found just in certain areas of the body. Dogs and cats, for example, can sweat only through the soles of their paws. At some point in human evolution we became an eccrine animal, with large numbers of these glands distributed over the entire body surface. I suggest that this glandular conversion had a profound influence in that it allowed the early human to become a hunter; in addition, it ultimately had an indirect influence on the kinds of infections we acquired during the long trudge to civilization.

When our first eccrine ancestors descended from the trees, they were confronted with the essential problem of all living creatures—getting a good, steady diet. The hot African savanna of that time was one huge meat market, but all the meat was on the hoof. And there was our puny human, unadorned with fang or claw, neither fleet of foot nor keen of senses.* This unspecialized creature had no way, all things being equal, to compete with the efficient large carnivores, such as the great cats and the hunting dogs. We made it, however, by the sweat of our brow. The apocrine carnivores had to limit their hunting to the cooler parts of the day. But our eccrine human could go out to hunt in the noonday sun. In effect, he could exploit an unoccupied ecological time-niche. With this start he was assured a diet of high-quality protein food. In time, human intelligence devised the prosthetic weaponry to make him an around-the-clock slayer.

Sweating, however, had its price. Since humans didn't develop any water-conservation mechanism—remaining unable, for instance, to concentrate urine, as does the camel—they were forever bound to a life near a water source. Even desert nomads are limited in their wanderings by the distance from oasis to oasis. As humans became more socialized they established their communities near permanent water sources—rivers, lakes, streams, and oases. Their activities became water oriented, and the human became not only a unique hunting primate but also a bathing primate, a fishing primate, and eventually, an agricultural primate.

So now we have people in intimate daily contact with water and forming larger and larger communities. Both

---

*However, if the attributes of early man resembled those of extant hunter-gatherers, he was in better sensory shape than the modern wage earner. Kalahari bushmen, for example, are said to be capable of seeing the four moons of Jupiter with the naked eye.

of these developments have played, and continue to play, an important role in determining the inventory of infectious diseases.

Many of our most serious and common infections are either water-borne or in some other way associated with water. Bound to water, we have been, and communities without a pure water supply still are, at high risk of acquiring those infections for which the pathogens, whether viruses, bacteria, or animal parasites, are present in drinking water. Cholera, typhoid fever, and amoebic dysentery are examples of life-threatening infections acquired by drinking contaminated water. Not as devastating but certainly of great concern to the afflicted are other largely water-borne infections, such as giardiasis (see chapter 13) and traveler's diarrhea, familiarly called Montezuma's revenge, Delhi belly, or simply *turista.*

Another group of pathogens with an enormous impact on human health can be considered water-associated. Many of the water-associated organisms are parasites, the *Plasmodium* of malaria being an example par excellence. Malaria cannot be contracted through drinking water. However, without the water that the mosquito vector requires during the larval stages there would be no malaria. Similarly, without the breeding water required by the blackfly vector of river blindness (see chapter 7) and without the habitat water of the snail vector of schistosomiasis (see chapter 8) these diseases would not exist.

The argument that sweating influenced community size, which in turn determined the kinds of infectious disease present, is somewhat convoluted, but logical nevertheless. The perspiration theory first takes us to the dawn of agriculture. It was quite late in the day before our sweating, water-bound humans realized that with a little effort a reliable food source, cultivated plants, could be raised on the frontage of their riverine or lakeside estates. This development of agriculture, some ten thousand years ago, induced further settlement, and except for a few remnant hunter-gatherers, we began to congregate into larger and larger communities.

The gradual improvement of agricultural methods resulted in more abundant crops and eventually in surplus food that could be bartered for other products. For barter, a centralized location was required, and market towns began to spring up. Also, the need for goods to be bartered stimulated manufacturing. And manufacturing led to the further growth of human groupings, which in time expanded into cities. The next step, according to the perspiration theory, involves the relationship between population size and infectious diseases (i.e., those caused by viral, bacterial, or animal parasites). We are saddened and indignant at reports of some isolated, remote tribal group brought to near-extinction by measles or whooping cough. These "childhood diseases," highly virulent for nonimmune adults, are unwittingly introduced by outsiders. And yet, outbreaks of these infections do not arouse the same alarm when they occur in our societies. That there is a difference in susceptibility is obvious; what is not so obvious is that community size not only determines the degree of susceptibility but also dictates which infections will be "normal" for a group and which will not.

Pathogenic organisms are as much elements of the ecosystem as are their hosts. A number of variables, including the density of the host population and the ability of the pathogen to persist in the host, govern whether or not a pathogen can be a customary component of the ecosystem. Some pathogens, such as the measles virus, have a short life span in the host. Normal host defenses against the measles virus are activated, particularly in children, to a degree that brings rapid self-cure. Following recovery the individual has a solid immunity to reinfection. For pathogens like the measles virus to persist in generation upon generation of humans, there must be a constantly replenished supply of nonimmunes; that is, the population must be large enough so that the number of nonimmunes is maintained by new births. It has been estimated that a community of 200,000 is necessary to keep the measles virus in circulation. On the other hand, only a small group is needed to perpetuate an infection if the pathogen persists in the host for a long time. Tuberculosis, malaria, and herpes simplex are examples of "small group" infections.

There is, however, a situation in which a pathogen with a brief infectious period survives even in a small community, one lacking the "critical mass"—the minimum number of hosts—such a pathogen would be expected to require. In cases of this kind a population of wild or domestic animals acts as the large group, the reservoir from which humans, incidentally, become infected. The infections transmitted from animals to humans are known as zoonoses; one good example is yellow fever, whose causative virus is normally found in the wild-monkey populations of Africa and tropical Latin America. F. L. Black has commented, "Only those organisms which, like varicella, can exist in small groups, and those which like yellow fever virus have a non-human reservoir, are likely to have played a role in the development of mankind through his much longer human history."

Finally, one aspect of the perspiration theory may account for the human's becoming, as Desmond Morris has said, a naked ape. A hairy body impedes evaporation and reduces the coolant efficiency of sweat. Therefore, once our ancestors began to perspire, there must have been a selective evolutionary pressure working in favor of the less hairy. The fact that Joe Weiner and I are bald has nothing whatsoever to do with this proposition.

3

ON NEW GUINEA
TAPEWORMS AND
JEWISH GRANDMOTHERS

Even I confess to a coolness of heart toward tapeworms. But when the World Health Organization calls, all parasites are equal, regardless of race or region. And so I recently found myself in the central highlands of Irian Jaya, Indonesian New Guinea, as a WHO consultant on the control of a pig-transmitted tapeworm that was sending a good many of the Ekari of Enarotali into epileptic-like convulsions. Once again I was about to learn that in problems of public health, expert but alien reason is usually not reasonable to the people of another culture.

For the peoples of New Guinea the pig is more than pork. Throughout the large island, man and pig have a relationship that is intimate beyond domesticity. The pig is a quasi family member, a source of food, and ultimately a gift to propitiate the spirit world. Gory festivals that feature the consumption of great numbers of pigs are held to gain prestige, to pay off obligations, or to celebrate a battle won. Pigs are in constant demand for ritual slaughter. One or more must be killed at the birth of a child or in any unfortunate circumstance or other perceived emergency requiring sacrifice to gods and ancestor spirits. Ritual slaughter represents something more than paying the premium for the insurance of good will: it reflects the absolute belief that life and sanity require harmony with the spirit world. Pig sacrifice is a major means of attaining that harmony. Hence, the introduction into New Guinea of the pork tapeworm, *Taenia solium,* was both a medical and a cultural disaster.

Pig and man share not only more habits than we like to admit but also two helminth parasites,* the nematode *Trichinella spiralis,* which causes trichinosis, and the tapeworm *Taenia solium.* Trichinosis, once common in the United States, can be an unpleasant, even fatal, infection; but in this piece the tapeworm is the villain.

The tapeworm is a gutless flatworm that absorbs nutrient directly through its body covering, or integument. In a sense, a tapeworm is a communal chain of individuals that keep in touch by means of common lateral nerve cords. Each mature segment in the chain comes complete with male and female sexual organs and an excretory pore to dispose of metabolic wastes.

The "head" of the tapeworm, a segment referred to as the scolex, has specialized structures—suckers, augmented in some species with hooks—to anchor the

*Parasitic invertebrates belonging to two phyla, Platyhelminthes and Nemathelminthes, are collectively referred to as worms or, more elegantly, as helminths. The platyhelminths include flukes and other flatworms (Trematoda, which are primitive animals lacking a mouth, a body cavity, and an anal opening to the digestive tract) and tapeworms (Cestoda, which have no digestive tract). The nemathelminths are cylindrical "wormy" creatures; they have a mouth and an anal opening to the digestive tract, and a type of body cavity known as a pseudocoelom.

worm to the host's intestinal wall. The scolex is also the germinal center from which the other segments of the tape arise. Near the scolex the segments are sexually immature; in the middle of the chain they are sexually functional; and at the terminal portion they are gravid—mere sacs of eggs. The gravid segments separate and either rupture and release their eggs inside the bowel or are passed whole with the feces.

To develop completely, a tapeworm requires one or more intermediate hosts. When a pig swallows the egg of a *Taenia* tapeworm, the egg hatches within the pig's intestine but does not develop into the adult tape. Instead, the microscopic embryo penetrates the intestinal wall and enters a small vein. Circulating blood carries the embryo to some part of the pig, where it develops into a bladderlike form (the cysticercus) with an invaginated structure that will eventually become the scolex. The tapeworm develops no further until a human ingests pork containing the cysticercus. Then, safe in its final home, the scolex pops out and attaches itself to the human intestinal wall, and the worm begins to grow to its full complement of segments.

Most tapeworms have a strict host-specific relationship; only man can serve as the definitive host (the host for the sexually mature stage) of *Taenia solium* and its close relative *Taenia saginata*. *T. solium* is known as the pork tapeworm and *T. saginata* as the beef tapeworm because the cysticerci are found respectively in the pig and in the cow.

Transmission of the disease occurs when infected humans defecate where cows or pigs feed. The animals ingest the eggs, which develop into cysticerci; and the cycle is completed when humans eat undercooked pork or tasty steak tartare. One highly important difference between the pork tapeworm and the beef tapeworm is that humans can also act as intermediate hosts for the pork tapeworm. If a person swallows eggs of the beef tapeworm, the worm embryos die. But if a human ingests eggs of the pork tapeworm, they can develop into the bladderlike cysticerci, causing a disease known as cysticercosis.

While harboring a twenty-foot tapeworm may not be a pleasure (except perhaps that you could refer to yourself in the imperial style as "We"), most infections of this type cause little discomfort. People harboring a tapeworm are often unaware of the beast within, unless they notice segments in their stools.

It is not the worms, but the cysticerci that can be devastatingly pathogenic. After hatching from the eggs and entering the blood system, the embryos frequently establish themselves in the brain, where they grow into the bladder form. In time, an inflammatory reaction can lead to such neurological disorders as epileptiform convulsions and bizarre personality changes mimicking psychosis. These pathogenic manifestations often do not appear until two to five years after a person has contracted the infection. The condition is like a time bomb inexorably ticking away in the brain.

In 1971 two physicians at the small Enarotali general hospital reported a bewildering "epidemic" of severe burns among the Ekari. Some of the twenty-five to thirty cases each month were so bad that limbs had to be amputated. All the patients gave similar accounts. While sleeping, they had been overcome by an epileptic seizure and had fallen unconscious into the household fire.

Enarotali is piercingly cold at night. The village sits on the shore of one of the Paniai Lakes (formerly called the Wissel Lakes) at an altitude of five thousand feet, surrounded by the wild barricade of the east-central mountain range. Hardly overdressed for this climate, the local Ekari men wear only a long gourd penis sheath and the women a brief string girdle. A fire in the center of each rude thatch hut wards off the night chill, and they sleep on bunks around the fire.

The hospital staff had treated accidental burns before 1971, but never on this scale. The frequency of the epileptiform attacks was also unusual, and the suspicion arose that some new infectious agent had been introduced.

The pathogen came to light during a survey for intestinal parasites by a team of scientists from the Department of Parasitology of the University of Indonesia School of Medicine in Djakarta. In 8 percent of the fecal samples they were astonished to find, along with the usual intestinal zoo, eggs of the tapeworm *Taenia*. Although many parasitological surveys had been carried out in New Guinea over the years, this finding was the first instance of taeniasis. Moreover, the diagnostic technique of microscopic examination of fecal specimens has a low sensitivity for this parasite. For example, in one African study only 6 percent of the stools showed taeniasis, while autopsy examinations indicated that more than 60 percent of the population had the tapeworm. So undoubtedly, many more cases existed.

Subsequent clinical examinations of the Ekari revealed cysts under the skin, a sign of heavy, disseminated cysticercosis, and the discovery of the deadly, pearly globules of the cysticerci studded in the brain of a patient who had died confirmed that these were the cause of the neurological syndrome. Serological tests performed by my Indonesian colleagues and me in

1978 indicate that at least 25 percent of the Ekari adults and children have cysticercosis.

But where did the parasite come from? How was it introduced into such a remote, isolated area? Reconstruction of historical events indicates that the tapeworm came unseen, riding the anticolonial wave; the vehicles of transport were men and pigs.

In 1969 the United Nations directed the peoples of West New Guinea to decide whether to join the Republic of Indonesia. The Ekari were uncertain, to say the least, about the change in regime, and during the plebiscite, or shortly thereafter, the Indonesians sent troops to Enarotali. Some of the soldiers came from Bali. Indonesia's President Suharto softened the military action by sending a gift of pigs. The pigs, too, came from Bali, the area in which pig rearing is largely concentrated, since Bali is Hindu and the rest of Indonesia is mostly Muslim.

Whatever the political and social advantages of the gift, the medical result was an unforeseen tragedy. The pork tapeworm has been endemic in Bali for at least sixty years. A favorite Balinese dish is an undercooked pork preparation in which the cysticerci are cleverly disguised by the legendary spices of the Indies. However, the Balinese are fastidiously clean in their personal habits, so although the tapeworm infection is prevalent, cysticercosis is almost nonexistent. In contrast, the Ekari have Stone Age toilet habits and when the tapeworm came from Bali, the Ekari became infected through both meat and human feces.

Transcultural tapeworm traffic hasn't been confined to the Bali–New Guinea route, and I should like to digress for a moment to recount a somewhat similar occurrence much closer to home. Now that it is epidemiological history, the story is rather amusing. It might be entitled "A Tapeworm Tale of Two Cities." The cast of characters includes the fish tapeworm, Scandinavian fishermen, and Jewish grandmothers in New York City.

The fish tapeworm is big, reaching a length of up to forty-five feet, and its name, *Diphyllobothrium latum*, fits its size. The historical endemic focus of *D. latum* is Scandinavia, where infected fishermen defecate into the lakes. The first intermediate host, a copepod, eats the egg. The second intermediate host, a fresh-water fish, eats the copepod. A wormlike larva develops in the muscles of the fish, and humans become infected by eating a Nordic version of sashimi.

When Scandinavian fishermen came to the United States during the nineteenth century, many settled in the lake region of Minnesota and Wisconsin, and there they began to practice their trade (and habits). Shortly thereafter the fish in these lakes became infected.

Commerce in live fish took place regularly between the Midwest and New York City, at least until the late 1930s. I recall that during my boyhood in New York almost every market had a large holding tank full of live pike, pickerel, and carp. The chief customers were Jewish housewives, who magically transformed the fish into an ambrosial concoction called gefilte fish.

Basically, gefilte fish is an amalgam of minced fish, pressed into balls, and boiled until done. "Until done" is the tricky part. The grandmothers of that time, by whom the thermometer was considered high technology, would sample the fish until it was cooked just right. The early samples were still quite raw and if infected, contained viable worm larvae. In this way, many a nice old lady of Gotham unwittingly acquired a forty-foot Scandinavian immigrant in her digestive tract. The introduction of fish inspection, sanitary practices, and thermometers, along with the gradual demise of the traditional Jewish grandmother's instinctive culinary arts, have made *D. latum* infections rare in the United States.

But to return from New York to highland New Guinea. By 1973 the main epidemiological factors governing the transmission of tapeworm disease were known, but the problem of control remained. In technically advanced countries, refrigerating the pork for the proper length of time kills the cysticerci. This is impossible in primitive Enarotali, but another effective method would be to cook the carcass thoroughly. Unfortunately, the traditional Ekari barbecue doesn't allow for thorough cooking. The Ekari throw the dead pig on the fire just long enough to warm it up. One reason for this haste is that, except at the big feasts, an Ekari wants the pig he slaughters to be all his. Neighbors are not customarily invited for dinner. The Ekari kills his pig secretly—or as secretly as a pig can be butchered—in the dead of night, following the kill with a quick turn on the fire. A fast-food meal takes place in stealth and gloom. (This and other customs have not endeared the Ekari to anthropologists, who have described them as greedy and avaricious, and as "primitive capitalists.")

Affliction with cysticercosis would seem a compelling enough reason to change cooking practice. With incontestable logic, the health educator from Djakarta, a dedicated woman trained at one of America's more prestigious schools of public health, tried to teach the new methods with all the zeal of a cordon bleu instructor. So there we were, the educator educating, the doctor expounding on the virtues of sanitation, and the Ekari nodding in pleasant agreement. After all, under the circumstances, who in his right mind could reject this appeal to common sense? Then one night it all fell apart and the cultural gap yawned into an abysmal chasm.

I was sitting by the fire drinking wine with the village elders. Through the translator, the chief expressed his bitterness that the disease introduced by foreigners had corrupted the tribe's pigs and religion. Then came the real shocker for me. He said: "We are not blind. We can see the seeds that give us the illness in the pig flesh. But no one lives forever, and if we must die, then we must die. Life is no longer a pleasure. We are only half men. The Indonesians will not let us make the warfare that gave us manhood. I no longer care if I eat the corrupt pig flesh.

"Even if this were not so, we still could not do as you say. You tell us not to eat the infected pig, to be careful, to cook it long. How can we do this? If a child is born at night we must sacrifice a pig immediately; there is no time to look and see if it has the seeds. The pig must be killed and eaten at once.

"When the missionaries brought us the coughing sickness many years ago [a whooping-cough epidemic in 1956], we rose in anger. This time we have no heart to do so."

After he concluded, the wine was passed around again. I couldn't remember ever having felt so lonely and helpless.

After I left Enarotali I flew to Djajapura, the provincial capital, to discuss the situation with the governor. He was highly sympathetic and concerned, particularly since we had clear evidence that the infection had now spread to other parts of Irian Jaya. We went over the possible remedies and the difficulty in implementing them, and as I was about to leave the governor's mansion he remarked, "You know, they are not like you and me. They are very primitive, and it is extremely difficult to change their customs even for their better health." I was about to agree when I noticed that we were both smoking cigarettes.

4

HOW THE WISE MEN
BROUGHT MALARIA
TO AFRICA

Once upon a time (but not too long ago) there lived a tribe deep within the Dark Continent. The people tilled the soil to raise crops of roots and grains, for they had little meat to lend them strength. Illness often befell them, but even so, in this dry land they were not overly troubled with the fever sickness brought by the mosquito. Now, in the Northern World there was a powerful republic that had compassion on these people and sent its Wise Men to relieve the mean burden of their lives. The Wise Men said, "Let them farm fish," and taught the people to make ponds and to husband a fish called tilapia.

The people learned well, and within a short time they had dug ten thousand ponds. The fish flourished, but soon the people could not provide the constant labor required to feed the fish and keep the ponds free of weeds. The fish became smaller and fewer, and into the ponds came the fever mosquitoes, which bred and multiplied prodigiously. The people then sickened and the children died from the fever that the medicine men from the cities called malaria. The Wise Men from the North departed, thinking how unfortunate it was that these people could not profit from their teachings. The people of the village thought it strange that Wise Men should be sent to instruct them in the ways of growing mosquitoes.

At about the same time, from 1957 to 1961, that this ecological misadventure was taking place in Kenya (for it was no fable), on the other side of the world the impoverished villagers of the Demerara River estuary in Guyana were enacting their own calamity. Striving to improve their lot by converting from subsistence farming of maize and cassava to cash-producing rice, they cleared the region for rice fields, displacing the livestock that had formerly abounded in villages. Mechanization on the roads and fields also progressed, bringing a further diminution in the number of domestic animals, particularly cattle and draft oxen.

The major potential carrier of malaria in the region was the mosquito *Anopheles aquasalis,* but since subsistence farming had created few suitable water collections for breeding, mosquitoes were present in only modest numbers. The wet rice fields, however, provided an ideal larval habitat and the vector population increased rapidly. Even so, all would have been well had there been no alteration in the livestock, since the genetically programmed behavior of *A. aquasalis* directs it to prefer blood meals from domestic animals rather than from humans. With the disappearance of the normal food supply, however, the hungry mosquitoes turned their attention to people. Intense mosquito–human contact now enhanced malaria transmission. And so the combination of rice and tractors contrived to bring malaria in epidemic proportions to the people of the Demerara River estuary.

The ecological disasters described in these two stories are not isolated phenomena. In the endemic regions of the tropics, many human activities create and multiply the breeding habitats of malaria-bearing mosquitoes. In their very attempts to break from the bondage of poverty, food shortage, and ill health, Third World peoples too often sow the seeds of disaster in the form of malaria.

Malaria of humans is caused by four species of a protozoan parasite* of the genus *Plasmodium*—*P. falciparum, P. vivax, P. malariae,* and *P. ovale.* While all four species can produce debilitating illness, only *P. falciparum* is sufficiently virulent to cause death. The complicated life cycle is, in the main, the same for all species. Two hosts are required—a human and a mosquito of the genus *Anopheles.* Infection in the human begins with the bite of the mosquito, which injects sporozoites, microscopic threadlike forms, into the host. The sporozoites enter the liver cells, where they divide. A single sporozoite may give rise asexually to as many as thirty thousand daughter cells. After a sojourn in the liver that may last from several weeks to months or even years,

---

*The organisms of the phylum Protozoa are single-celled animals. Within their life unit are performed all the functions carried out by the concerted effort of the specialized tissues of the pluralistic society that is the multicellular animal. Protozoa include the amoebae, which move by "blobbing" about; the flagellates, which move by means of one or more propelling whiplike filamentous structures; the ciliates, whose external surfaces bear short, hairlike structures that move in unison to "row" the organisms in their fluid environment; and the sporozoa (among them the malaria parasites), which are parasites with a complex life cycle involving both asexual and sexual reproductive phases.

depending on the species and strain of parasite, the cells (merozoites) are released into the blood stream, where they invade the red blood cells.

Within the red blood cells the parasites grow and divide, much as they did in the liver phase, each ultimately producing asexually ten to sixteen daughter cells. The red blood cell finally bursts, freeing the daughter cells (merozoites) to invade other red blood cells. Since the cycle is synchronous, it causes periodically recurrent episodes of chills and fever—the hallmarks of malaria.

Several days after the onset of the blood phase, new, sexual forms appear within the red blood cells. These are the male and female gametocytes. They undergo no further change until ingested by the feeding mosquito. A marvelously adaptive process has evolved in which the gametocytes are mature and infective to the mosquito for only a short period of the day. This period of infectivity occurs at night, the time when most anopheline carriers take their blood meal.

In the mosquito stomach the gametocytes are transformed into male and female gametes and fertilization occurs. The fertilized female gamete penetrates the mosquito stomach wall, coming to rest on the exterior surface. There it forms a cystlike body, the oocyst. Within this cyst intense cytoplasmic reorganization and nuclear division take place, and as many as ten thousand sporozoites form. The maturation of the oocyst requires seven to fourteen days, depending on temperature and other factors. Upon maturation it bursts, releasing the sporozoites, which invade the mosquito's salivary glands. The mosquito can now infect a hqman when next it feeds.

The anopheline mosquito is the critical link in perpetuating the malaria parasite, and the nature of the contact between human and mosquito greatly influences the level of endemicity. An important factor of this relationship is the life cycle of the mosquito in interaction with its environment. Each anopheline species has characteristic biological and behavioral traits that determine its interaction with man and other hosts. The mosquito's preference for a specific type of breeding water and a specific host upon which to feed, and the mosquito's resting behavior, are genetically controlled characteristics, which may or may not place a particular species in proximity to man. In many regions of the tropics, human activities, particularly those associated with agriculture, have altered the environment, producing suitable breeding sites and increasing the likelihood of human contact with malaria mosquitoes.

Of the agricultural practices that alter the natural tropical ecosystem, rice culture is one of the most important in creating optimal conditions for malaria transmission. Rice farming requires large, open areas of water, the preferred habitat of many of the most efficient anopheline carriers of malaria. This open water is found especially in new rice fields, where the young plants are placed well apart. Also, the generation time of the mosquito is reduced in the sun-elevated temperature of the exposed water, and breeding is prolific. In addition, a relatively large body of standing water increases the humidity of the surrounding biosphere, and the higher humidity prolongs the mosquito's life. The longer a mosquito lives, the more people it bites.

A vicious series of events may develop, beginning with the intense vector–human contact. Because rice culture is seasonal, peak densities of mosquitoes generally occur for relatively short periods. The limited transmission period prevents the development of a protective immunity. At the same time, when farmers are incapacitated by malaria during the planting season, crop production suffers, leading to economic loss and shortage of food.

Ecological changes of the kind just described have been excellently documented in a study of Kenya's Kano Plain rice-development scheme. Prior to establishment of the rice plots, the Kano Plain landscape was characterized by villages of scattered huts, maize farms interspersed with seasonal swamps and water holes in which pistia plants grew. In this unmodified environment, 99 percent of the mosquitoes were of the genus *Mansonia*, a nonvector of malaria, while only 1 percent were *Anopheles gambiae*. After the land was modified for rice farming, 65 percent of the mosquitoes were *A. gambiae* and 28 percent *Mansonia* (the other 7 percent were of another variety). Similar alterations in mosquito populations following the introduction of rice farming have occurred in such diverse areas of the world as Venezuela, Tanzania, India, Syria, and Morocco (where until 1949 the French colonial government had, for health reasons, banned rice growing).

In the tropical world the ecosystem undergoing the most rapid and extensive alterations for human purposes is the forest. These alterations have frequently resulted in an increase in malaria, often out of all proportion to the small degree of disturbance created.

Within the intact tropical rain forest there are relatively few species of mosquitoes that transmit human malaria. The forest provides few permanent or semipermanent accumulations of water, also, the main anopheline carriers prefer sunlit breeding sites and avoid shade. But just such sites abound when the forest is cleared by the farmer digging a plot of ground, by the lumberer using tractors and other machines, and by the builders of the rutted roads used to service the new settlements.

Conversely, on at least one occasion, the creation of a forest has led to problems. When the cacao industry was begun in Trinidad, a man-made forest of immortelle trees was planted to provide the shade required by cacao plants. Certain South and Central American anophelines, showing the remarkable specialization a mosquito species may have, breed exclusively in water contained in the bromeliad epiphytes* of the forest gallery. When bromeliads colonized the high immortelle trees, *A. bellator* proliferated, carrying malaria to the plantation workers and their families.

In an attempt to solve their problems—overcrowded cities, land shortage and the need for establishing a market economy—political and technical authorities in the developing countries have opened new land to agricultural development. Such projects commonly begin with the clearing of the jungle, followed by resettlement of transmigrants and the cultivation of cash crops, such as cotton, tobacco, rice, and corn. But all too frequently, the ecological alterations brought about by deforestation, the creation of irrigation systems, and other human activities enhance the vector population. More often than not, the settlers brought into the area have had little exposure to malaria and have not acquired sufficient immunity to protect them from severe attacks. For example, within eight months of leaving nonmalarious urban centers in Java for an agricultural project in

*Epiphytes are plants that derive their nutriment from rain and air; they often grow on other plants. Bromeliads are tropical American plants that are mostly epiphytes.

South Sulawesi, 32 percent of the settlers were stricken with malaria, and the enterprise nearly collapsed.

The ability to protect the settlers by chemical control of the anopheline carrier has often been negated by prior use of agricultural insecticides, such as DDT. Spraying crops to protect against the ravages of destructive insects and spraying for the control of the anopheline vector involve different and generally incompatible techniques. Where insecticide has been broadcast for crop protection, the anopheline population receives sublethal doses that eventually render it physiologically or behaviorally resistant. Thus, by the time antimalaria measures are instituted, the avenue of mosquito control by chemical means has been closed.

Cost accounting of ecological alteration is difficult, particularly when the influence of a single factor, malaria, must be traced through a complicated mosaic of interacting elements. One excellent exercise in ecological-economic sleuthing was carried out by the Pan American Health Organization after new land had been opened for agricultural development in Paraguay. In the first year, malaria seriously afflicted the settlers and the impact of the disease reduced the over-all production of cash crops—tobacco, cotton, and corn—by 36 percent. Worker efficiency, particularly during the harvest, which coincided with the height of the malaria season, was reduced by as much as 33 percent. Debilitated by malaria, the farmers devoted their limited energy to their cash crops, abandoning all of the subsistence crops except the easily cultivated, but starchy, manioc. As a result, nutritional deterioration was added to the burden of malaria.

In subsequent years there was reduced expansion of farms in the malaria-struck region. Tragically, by the time the Paraguayan government and its advisers became aware of the health hazards, a large amount of capital had been expended on land development, and the government had too little left in the kitty to secure the "beachhead" by providing the infrastructure of health, education, and other social services. The Paraguayan experience has been repeated throughout the tropics.

In addition to developing agriculture, Third World governments have expanded electric-power resources in their attempts to promote economic development. But along with the kilowatts, rice, and fish, these giant hydroelectric and water-impoundment schemes have also produced malaria. The seepages and canals have provided optimal breeding habitats for malaria mosquitoes in such geographically diverse projects as the Aswan High Dam in Egypt, the Kariba project in Zambia, the Lower Seyhan project in Turkey, and early in its history, the TVA scheme in the United States. On occasion, the dams and man-made lakes were not in themselves responsible for ecological change leading to intensified malaria transmission, but, rather, set in motion a train of events that led to the situation. Construction of the Kalimawe Dam in Tanzania, for example, enabled farmers to put more of their land under cultivation, and as a result, their cattle—the preferred host of the local *A. gambiae*—had to be grazed farther from the villages. When the cattle were no longer kept near the houses at night, the mosquitoes turned their attention to the human inhabitants, and the incidence of malaria increased.

Ecological alterations have been caused not only by man's struggles toward progress but also by his conflicts; throughout history the environment has been a casualty of war. This ecological havoc has often created conditions conducive to malaria transmission in both temperate and tropical regions, and epidemics have victimized military personnel and civilians.

During World War II, for example, the bloody fighting near Cassino, Italy, destroyed dikes containing the rivers. Anopheline mosquitoes bred profusely in the flooded areas and bomb craters. Malaria, possibly introduced by foreign troops, occurred in its most violent form, with some villages totally infected and suffering a mortality rate of 10 percent.

But it was in the Vietnam conflict that a new and devastating tactical strategy was applied: the ecosystem became a deliberate target of massive destruction. The use of aircraft-spread herbicides for the defoliation of forests and the destruction of crops introduced a new dimension to the horror of war. Scientists throughout the world were alarmed, and a number of studies were conducted to determine the consequences of defoliation.

One such study, that of the congressionally funded National Academy of Sciences committee, included an investigation of ecological-epidemiological interactions in defoliated forests in Vietnam. Among these was a defoliated mangrove forest south of Saigon known as the Rung Sat. This area, repeatedly sprayed with herbicide, had become a desolate, barren wasteland denuded of virtually every living tree. An intact mangrove forest was studied as a control, and the NAS medical ecologists did not detect in it any breeding sites of anopheline mosquitoes. Other mosquitoes were abundant, but the Southeast Asian mangrove ecosystem was not suitable for anophelines. In the Rung Sat, however, the mosquito population consisted largely of *A. sinensis* and *A. lesteri*. Malaria was endemic throughout the region.

Again, rice seems to have been the final ecological culprit. When people could no longer obtain their livelihood from woodcutting, they turned to rice culture in the less saline areas of the dead mangrove forest. The rice fields provided ideal breeding sites for the two anopheline species.

In Vietnam the main foci of malaria are in the hill and mountainside forests, the vectors being *A. maculatus,* which breeds in exposed hillside streams, and *A. balabacensis,* which lives in sunlit standing collections of water. Removal of the forests' shade created new breeding sites for these mosquitoes. The fighting in Vietnam prevented the NAS committee from doing research on the ground in the highlands, but when the group flew over the deforested mountain areas, they saw the kind of landscape typically colonized by these two efficient vectors. And American soldiers fighting in the Vietnam highland forests were indeed severely afflicted with malaria, the attack rate in some units being as high as 53 cases per 1,000 troops per day.

Paradoxically and cruelly, in the absence of an effective control program, a community's welfare and stability often depend on continuous, intense exposure to malaria. Under these conditions, as in the agricultural villages of Africa and Southeast Asia, malaria causes high infant mortality; some 40 percent or more of the children under the age of five may die of the infection. Those who survive, however, develop a protective immunity, so the adults, the productive segment of the community, remain relatively free of the pernicious clinical manifestations of the infection. Usually, a high birthrate compensates for the high infant mortality, and a population equilibrium is achieved in which the workers are sufficiently healthy to produce the community's food.

The relatively slow acquisition of functional immunity to malaria, and its concomitant cost in infant life, have led to several disasters of good intent and have presented new moral dilemmas for discomfited public-health workers. The moral dilemmas arise because health professionals trained in the West have held, by tradition and education, a philosophy affirming the importance of individual human life and the right of every member of the community to good health. The heroic efforts begun in the mid-1950s to realize global eradication of malaria were rooted in this moral premise. But where these control programs were successful in the developing tropical countries, the population increased rapidly, while technical-agricultural resources to accommodate the burgeoning community lagged sadly behind. Following a successful control scheme in Guyana, infant mortality was reduced to one-third its former rate; in one study group, a sugar plantation village, the population rose from the precontrol level of 66,000 in 1957 to 110,000 in 1966. Some students of public health, as well as health officials, are now beginning to question the wisdom of instituting such measures as malaria control unless they are accompanied by effective population-control programs or by expansion of resources to feed, clothe, educate, and house the increased population.

The disasters of good intent are related to malaria's tendency to return several years after the completion of a successful mosquito-control program. During this period the mosquito populations regain their former density, while the human population's collective immunity wanes. Wherever malaria recurs under these circumstances, it is explosive and clinically severe.

It is doubtful whether progress for the peoples of the developing world, as we define progress, can be achieved unless malaria and other diseases draining their intellectual and physical energies can be brought under control. Yet the enterprises of progress contribute, with monotonous regularity, to the deterioration of health. What is now required is a holistic approach. Engineers, agronomists, epidemiologists, economists, ecologists, demographers, cultural anthropologists, and political leaders must all contribute to the planning, execution, and evaluation processes. In this way, malaria and many other diseases can be reduced to a manageable state if not actually eradicated. Human needs demand it; human intelligence and ingenuity must be turned to achieving a degree of progress, rather than disaster, for the peoples of the Third World.

5

·

THE BEAN, THE GENE,
AND MALARIA

She was only eight years old, but suffered with a stoic resignation that was as poignant as her desperate condition. She had experienced similar crises of nausea, vomiting, and piercing joint pains many times before. The medical team of the central city's hospital worked with rapid efficiency. Within a few minutes of her admission, the metal tree stood next to her bed, holding bottles of the blood and the glucose and salt solutions that were being slowly transfused into her fragile veins. In other patients, under similar circumstances, a surgeon's evaluation for a possible acute abdominal condition would have been called for immediately. But this child's records were at hand, and the attending phsycian was not misled by the clinical mimicry in her symptoms. Clearly, his young patient was undergoing a crisis of sickle-cell anemia. The child was black, and her blood abnormality was the product of a bargain evolution has struck with the most malignant of the malaria parasites infecting humans, *Plasmodium falciparum*. For the approximately ninety thousand American blacks afflicted with sickle-cell anemia and the three million asymptomatic carriers of the defective gene—all of them, unlike their ancestors, not at risk to malaria—it is no longer a bargain.

In a constantly changing, competitive world the Natural Selection Agreement gives a species no alternative but to adapt or perish. An environment becomes drier, and the plants better able to withstand desiccation survive and proliferate. A new, virulent pathogen is introduced, and the life forms that possess better defenses— a more alert immune system, a thicker skin, a composition that makes them less nutritious for the pathogen— have a survival advantage over the more susceptible. These characteristics, like all the properties of a living organism—are determined by a chemically coded genetic tape, the DNA double-stranded helix. From time to time, in one organism or another, the code alters in a seemingly random fashion to produce mutants. Selective pressures, such as those just mentioned, determine whether or not these mutants will continue their line.

Clearly, malaria can be expected to exert a potent selective pressure, with mutants possessing enhanced resistance to malaria favored to survive and reproduce. The immune response to malaria is relatively inefficient in children, so unless they were protected by other factors they are likely to die before they reach reproductive age. Moreover, acquired immunity in the adult female is depressed during pregnancy. Malaria during this critical time not only threatens the mother's life but is also an important cause, in highly endemic regions, of fetal death. The infants who *are* born of malarious mothers have a lower birth weight than infants with uninfected mothers and are less likely to survive.

Less is known about malaria's effect on male fertility, but earlier malariologists, such as John Sinton (a remarkable man who was recipient of Great Britain's two most coveted honors, fellowship of the Royal Society and the Victoria Cross), were convinced that it impaired male fertility, particularly during the season when transmission was at its height. Although unsupported by experimental proof, these earlier observations have a certain logic. The frequent relapses and reinfections with all forms of malaria that are experienced by semi-immunes living in an endemic setting may not be severely pathogenic, but they do induce fever. Even the "benign" *P. vivax* can raise temperature to 104°F. Sperm can't stand the heat, and the prolonged fever in affected adult males can be expected to reduce their fertility. Therefore, any mutations that confer even a partially protective innate resistance (since the degree of fever and the severity of the disease are directly related to the number of circulating parasites) will be favored to persist in the population.

For several of these protective mutations nature has imposed a cruel price. Genetic mutations produced abnormal, physiologically defective hemoglobin (the oxygen-carrying pigment of red blood cells) that was protective against malaria. When evolution's balance came to rest, the protective advantage outweighed the physiological disability, and the defective genes became established in the population. The relationship between abnormal hemoglobin and innate resistance to malaria is particularly evident in the case of sickle-cell anemia.

Sickle-cell anemia has been recognized as a disease entity for many years, but not until 1949 were its genetic basis and molecular mechanisms worked out. In that year J. V. Neel, in the United States, and E. A. Beet, in South Africa, independently showed that a man and woman who do not display any sign of the disease may have a child with sickle-cell anemia. Nor do the red blood cells of such parents have the abnormal, sickle-shaped form characteristic of the anemic state. Not until these red blood cells are experimentally placed in an atmosphere with an oxygen content less than that of air does their difference from truly normal red blood cells become apparent. When deprived of oxygen, the parents' red blood cells assume the sickle shape of the cells of their affected child, whereas normal cells do not change shape under these conditions. When family histories were traced it became evident that sickle-cell anemia was a genetic disease, inherited according to the laws formulated by Friar Gregor Mendel for his famous peas.

All animals and plants that reproduce sexually are, in the genetic sense, the expressed sum of two interacting sets of genes—one set from the mother, the other from the father. Each interacting gene pair controls a single characteristic—eye color, the presence of an antigenic determinant, the chemical composition of hemoglobin. With this in mind let us examine the inheritance of sickle-cell anemia. The gene pair of each of the asymptomatic parents consists of one gene that issues instructions for normal hemoglobin to be formed and one that issues instructions for sickle-cell hemoglobin. Hence, all the red blood cells of each parent contain a mixture of the two kinds of hemoglobin, resulting in a condition known as sickle-cell *trait*. Fortunately, in people with sickle-cell trait the "bad" hemoglobin is mixed with enough "good" hemoglobin to make the red blood cells essentially free of disease, although there is some risk that blood clots will develop at high altitudes in insufficiently pressurized aircraft. When two people with

sickle-cell trait have children, the same law of chance
applies that operates in crap shooting. The accompanying figure shows what the probabilities are. There are
two chances in four that the offspring will have sickle-
cell trait, one chance in four that it will have entirely
normal hemoglobin, and one chance in four that it will
receive a double defective-gene dose—that both genes
will be encoded for the abnormal hemoglobin, and it
will therefore suffer from sickle-cell *anemia*.

		Mother	
		A*	S
Father	A	AA (normal)	AS (sickle-cell trait)
	S	AS (sickle-cell trait)	SS (sickle-cell anemia)

*A stands for the normal hemoglobin gene and S for the sickle-cell gene.

The coding error caused by the defective gene is so
slight that not until 1957, when the appropriate technology became available, did the chemical difference
between normal hemoglobin and sickle-cell hemoglobin
become apparent. Hemoglobin is a chain of 279 amino
acids, joined in orderly sequence. Iron atoms attached
to the chain give it its oxygen-carrying capacity. Sickle-
cell anemia is caused by a change in only one of the 279
amino acids, with glutamic acid being replaced by
valine. The variation seems so trivial that it prompted

V. M. Ingram, the British scientist who discovered this chemical difference, to remark that "a change of one amino acid in nearly 300 is a small change indeed and yet this slight alteration can be fatal to the unfortunate possessor of the errant hemoglobin." And the effect of this coding error is indeed disastrous. The sickle-cell hemoglobin is inefficient in acquiring oxygen and is reluctant to release the oxygen that it has captured. The presence of sickle-cell hemoglobin also reduces the flexibility of the red blood cells, thereby impeding the cells' passage through the small blood vessels. The red blood cells tend to aggregate, and the aggregations—thrombi—cause multiple hemorrhages. In addition, the life of the red blood cell in sickle-cell anemia is much shorter than that of the normal red blood cell, and this too contributes to the chronic anemia. When palliative treatment is not given (there is no cure at present) the life span of the victim is abbreviated; few survive beyond the age of ten. Even those who are treated cannot expect to live beyond thirty-five or forty. The paradox of sickle-cell anemia is that the defective gene has survived in affected populations for many hundreds, and probably thousands, of years. Logic suggests that there should have been a selective "culling out" of the gene over a period of evolutionary time.

The evolutionary "reason" for sickle-cell hemoglobin began to come to light in 1954, when Tony Allison, working in England and Africa, looked at the geographic distribution of the abnormal gene. He noted that it is mainly confined to tropical Africa, where up to 45 percent of the individuals in some tribes have sickle-cell trait and about 3 percent of the children suffer from sickle-cell anemia. The gene is also present in the negroid Veddoid aboriginals of India, the Achdam of southern Arabia, and, to a lesser extent, in some Mediterranean peoples, particularly the Greeks. The bells of logic began to ring for Allison when he compared the distribution of the gene to that of *P. falciparum* malaria and noted a remarkably coincidental pattern. However, when Allison and other investigators carried out epidemiological studies to prove their theory, they were confused by the finding that the percentage of people with *P. falciparum* in their blood was as high for those with sickle-cell trait as for those with normal hemoglobin. Not until hospital cases were studied did the protective effect of sickle-cell trait become evident. In Africa, malaria is one of the chief causes for the hospitalization of children. But of the children hospitalized because of malaria, hardly any were found to have sickle-cell trait. Almost all of the children suffering from severe *P. falciparum* malaria had normal hemoglobin. Study after study confirmed these initial findings. Apparently, then, although sickle-cell trait does not completely protect against the infection it does limit it. For some reason that is still not clear, the malaria parasites fail to thrive in red blood cells containing some sickle-cell hemoglobin, and their multiplication (and, therefore, their pathogenic effect) is restricted. Tragically, the children with sickle-cell anemia do not receive even this protective benefit. When these children become infected with *P. falciparum*, the parasites, even at low density, often provoke a sickle-cell crisis and the children die from the combined effects of the crisis and the malaria. Some years ago I accompanied a young, dedicated Nigerian physician on his rounds of a pediatric ward in a hospital in southern Nigeria, and I recall him saying, "You know, in time malaria will be controlled in Africa and these beds [of the children with malaria] will be empty, but these other beds [of the children with sickle-cell anemia] will continue to be occupied, and the disease will continue to be a major health problem of my country's children long after malaria has disappeared."

Students of African history, medical anthropology, and malariology have attempted to limn a picture of the interacting effects of malaria, the sickle-cell gene, and the development of agriculture in Africa. It is believed that two thousand years ago the early blacks lived at the edge of the great tropical rain forests of West and Central Africa. At that time they still roamed the forest and bordering savanna in small bands of hunter-gatherers. The gene for sickle-cell hemoglobin was probably not present, or if present was very rare, since it would have enjoyed little selective advantage. In the then undisturbed ecological settings of forest and savanna, there were doubtless few breeding sites for the eminently efficient malaria vector *Anopheles gambiae*. Presumably, these people were essentially malaria-free. Several hundred years before the birth of Christ two events occurred that were to permanently change the face of Africa. The first was the introduction of new root and tree crops—yams, taros, bananas, and coconuts. These plants were brought to East Africa by the incredibly accomplished Malayo-Polynesian sailors who journeyed from Southeast Asia in their great double-hulled sailing canoes. One evidence of this early contact is that the language spoken in Madagascar can still be understood by the Man-anyan group of Borneo.

It was during this time that the second event occurred: the sickle-cell gene made its debut in Africa. It may have arisen as a spontaneous mutation in an indigenous tribal group, or it may, as some scholars suggest, have been introduced by migrating Achdam of southern Arabia, who crossed into Africa by way of the narrow strait at the southern end of the Red Sea. Or it may have come through contact with the Veddoids of India, who are believed to have wandered into Africa. But whatever the source, the sickle-cell gene and the taro made an outstandingly successful combination. The taro and the yam are highly suitable for cultivation in the humid tropical forest. The African peoples quickly adopted these new root crops, and in a few hundred years they had cleared an extensive tract of rain forest, extending in a wide belt from coast to coast. In doing so the farmers of the forest created numerous breeding sites for the mosquito *A. gambiae*, and if not for the sickle-cell gene, the penetration of the forest and the extended human colonization of Africa would probably have been aborted. Under the new conditions of hyperendemic malaria, the aberrant gene was favored; it is estimated that within thirty-five generations the proportion of those with the sickle-cell gene (i.e., sickle-cell trait) rose from 0.1 percent to 45 percent of the population in the groups at greatest risk to malaria. Now there was a double feedback. The protective effect of sickle-cell trait freed a significant part of the population from the debilitating effects of malaria, thereby releasing a quantum of human energy that could be directed to growing still more crops. The relatively plentiful food, along with the reduction of morbidity and mortality due to malaria, removed the barriers to population growth. And as population swelled, habits and social institutions changed. These peoples became settled farmers, and with population growth there was a centripetal attraction to gather into larger and larger groups. Agricultural villages grew into towns, and in time some of the towns became cities. By the twelfth century, perhaps sooner, the sickle-cell gene and the root crops had done their work, and the truly primeval phase of Africa was over.

Several other genetically controlled, inherited, abnormalities of the red blood cells are also believed to confer some degree of innate resistance to malaria. One of these, known as G-6-PD deficiency, is not a hemoglobin defect, as in sickle cell, but rather a condition in which the concentration of the enzyme glucose-6-phosphate dehydrogenase is abnormally low in the red blood cells. G-6-PD plays an important role in red-blood-cell metabolism, promoting the first step in the breakdown of glucose for energy.

As in the case of sickle-cell trait, attention was first drawn to the possible relationship between G-6-PD deficiency and malaria by their similar distributions. However, G-6-PD deficiency is present in a much greater diversity of peoples than is the sickle-cell gene. G-6-PD deficiency is relatively common in peoples of tropical Africa, Asia, the Middle East, the Mediterranean region, and Melanesia. Also, while the case for the protective effect of sickle-cell trait is now well established, that for G-6-PD deficiency is still controversial. The clinical data are conflicting. In some parts of the world, such as Africa, the evidence that people with G-6-PD deficiency control their *P. falciparum* better than those with normal red-blood-cell enzyme activity is equivocal at best. In other parts of the world, such as Greece and Sardinia, the claim for a protective effect rests on a somewhat firmer clinical foundation. These differences are probably due to the fact that unlike sickle-cell hemoglobin, which results from the coding error of a single gene, G-6-PD deficiency seems to be under the control of a number of genes. Seventy-eight genetically different variants of G-6-PD deficiency have been identified, and these seem to provide differing levels of protection against malaria. Nor do we have a clear understanding of how the enzyme deficiency may have a deleterious effect on the parasite. Under experimental culture conditions simulating the normal physiological state of the body, invading *P. falciparum* parasites grew in red blood cells deficient in G-6-PD just as well as in normal cells. Only when the red blood cells were deprived of oxygen did a difference appear: the parasites continued to grow in oxygen-deprived normal cells, but failed to thrive in those that were enzyme-deficient.

In any event, except for a slight anemia in some cases of some variants, G-6-PD deficiency does not cause any clinical manifestations. However, there is a health hazard associated with it. When people with G-6-PD deficiency are exposed to certain substances, they develop a condition known as intravascular hemolysis, in which the red blood cells tend to disrupt. The sulfonamides and the antimalarial drug primaquine are two of the substances that trigger this hemolysis and therefore cannot be given to individuals with red blood cells deficient in G-6-PD. But the most powerful inducer of this hemolysis is the fava bean (*Vicia faba*), also known as the broad bean. The resulting hemolytic condition, known as favism, can be so devastating as to be fatal within hours after a person with G-6-PD deficiency inhales the pollen of the plant or within one to two days after such a person eats its beans.

Despite this risk, the fava bean has for hundreds of years been a staple food of peoples with a high proportion of G-6-PD deficiency. It's not that these peoples have failed to recognize the bean's effect. The anthropologist Alfred Andrews has noted that "no plant or animal known to the Indo-Europeans has produced a more luxuriant growth of beliefs than fava beans." Admittedly, every culture has its share of food faddists; but even so, why would any group of people continue to grow and consume fava beans, knowing full well that this diet would cause 10 percent to 50 percent of their number to become ill, sometimes seriously ill? Common sense would dictate that where a large part of a population carried the G-6-PD deficiency gene, either the people would forgo the bean, or the carriers would be at a disadvantage and eventually selective pressure would eliminate the gene from the gene pool. But this has not happened; both gene and bean have become stabilized in these populations. And this brings us back, by a rather circuitous route, to malaria. Medical scientists and historians, intrigued by this genetic-dietary paradox, have searched for a factor that would make consumption of the bean more of an advantage than a disadvantage. Three attributes of the populations in question were discerned: (1) they grew and consumed fava beans; (2) they included a high proportion of people with the gene for G-6-PD deficiency; and (3) they were, or had been in the not too distant past, subject to moderate to high malaria endemicity. Could the malaria somehow have caused the persistence of gene and bean? Recent studies indicate that this may have been the case.

First, it has been found that fava beans contain a substance, vicine, which in chemical composition is remarkably similar to a highly effective antimalarial drug, pyrimethamine. The fava bean may thus have a direct antimalarial action, and its continued consumption may afford a certain amount of prophylactic protection. Second, the fava bean may have provided an extra degree of protection against malaria in individuals with red blood cells deficient in G-6-PD. We saw earlier that experimental studies with test-tube cultures showed that parasite growth was inhibited in red blood cells deficient in G-6-PD only when the amount of oxygen present was abnormally low—that is, under conditions of oxydant stress. The hemolysis-inducing drugs and the fava bean produce chemicophysical changes in these red blood cells that are similar to the changes produced by oxydant stress. It may be that these people learned to eat just enough fava beans to induce the protective state in their red blood cells but not to induce hemolysis and the resultant anemia.

Evolution's biological audit proved that the human species was better able to survive with the inherited red-blood-cell abnormalities than with *P. falciparum* malaria. Nature has, however, given one "antimalarial" genetic endowment which does not force the recipients to accept the bad in order to avoid the worse. For many years malariologists were perplexed by the fact that West Africans are solidly resistant to infection with *P. vivax*, the cause of benign tertian malaria. *P. falciparum, P. malariae,* and *P. ovale* are all present in West Africans, but there has never been a confirmed case of *P. vivax,* although this infection is common in all other parts of the malarious world. Several experimental attempts have been made to infect West African blacks with *P. vivax,* but not a single parasite has ever appeared in the blood of these volunteers. The mystery was finally solved by the elegant studies of Louis Miller and his colleagues at the National Institutes of Health. Miller reasoned that since malaria parasites live within the host cells, the factor that makes the red blood cells refractory to infection with *P. vivax* should be found in or on those cells; that is, the red blood cells of West African blacks should differ in at least one respect from those of all other peoples. Since the first barrier to invasion that confronts the malaria parasite is the outer membrane of the red blood cell, Miller's starting point was to examine antigens present on the outer surface of this membrane. These surface antigens are the inherited, genetically determined blood-group factors. The major antigens, of the OAB blood-group system, are familiar to all whose blood has had to be cross-matched for transfusion. There are also many minor antigenic determinants; these will be more familiar to the person who has had the misfortune to be involved in a paternity suit.

When Miller compared the whole array of blood-group antigens of West Africans with those of other peoples, he found one conspicuous difference. A red-cell-membrane antigen known as Duffy antigen was present on all the red blood cells except those of West Africans and American blacks of West African origin. Miller and his colleagues hypothesized that the absence of the Duffy antigen made the West Africans insusceptible to *P. vivax* infection. But how? All other factors responsible for innate resistance to malaria, such as sickle-cell hemoglobin and G-6-PD deficiency, do not prevent parasite invasion; it is conditions *within* the abnormal red cell that retard (but do not completely prevent) the growth and multiplication of *P. falciparum.* To answer this question they turned from theory to experiment. A motion picture was made through the microscope of what happened to a malaria parasite (that of a congruent monkey malaria, *P. knowlesi,* in their initial experiments) as it interacted, in a culture, with red blood cells. They mixed the merozoites, the minute stage of the malaria parasite that invades the red blood cells, with Duffy-negative blood in one sample and

Duffy-positive blood in another. The resulting movie was as exciting to scientists as any Academy Award winner would be to the general public. It showed the merozoites attaching by their anterior end to the surface of the Duffy-positive cells preparatory to invasion. With a thrusting motion they indented the surface, and then the cell membrane enfolded them and they penetrated into the red blood cells. In the mixture of merozoites and Duffy-negative blood, the cinephotomicrograph revealed a different scenario being enacted under the microscope. The merozoites displayed the same dancing movement as they sought red blood cells to invade. However, when the merozoites made contact with the Duffy-negative cells they did not become attached to the surface membrane, but actually bounced back, as if repelled. Invasion did not take place, and the merozoites, whose extracellular life span is brief, died.

These experiments not only illuminated the mechanism responsible for the West African's innate immunity to *P. vivax* but also introduced a new concept of how the malaria parasite invades the red blood cell. It would appear that the surface membrane of the red blood cell has chemical receptors of specific configuration into which the merozoite's complementary receptors must fit before invasion can occur. It is rather like a spaceship docking with Skylab. In the case of *P. vivax* the red-blood-cell receptor is the Duffy antigen or a receptor site closely associated with it. Unless the *P. vivax* first "docks" with the Duffy antigen, the second step—actual penetration into the host cell—cannot take place.

The receptor antigens for other malaria parasites, notably *P. falciparum*, have not as yet been identified, but they are probably there, awaiting revelation by the appropriate experimental probe. Miller is excited by the prospect that he can isolate each merozoite's specific receptor and use it as a vaccine to produce what should be a solid immunity. That isolation will be a very tricky business, but he speaks enthusiastically of exploiting the new, remarkable techniques utilizing hybridomas (certain kinds of tumor cells made into producers of specific antibodies by fusion with antibody-producing white blood cells) and recombinant-DNA technology. I'm a rather old-fashioned malariologist, and I tell Lou, who is a close personal friend, that this is Buck Rogers stuff. But in my secret heart I wish I had done those experiments.

6

•

THE FLY THAT
WOULD BE KING

One African tyrant does not attend political councils, is
not a member of the Organization of African Unity, and
has not palavered with roving diplomats, and does have
a personal air-transport system—the tsetse. Holding
Africa in thralldom since ancient times, this parasite,
known as a trypanosome, is only six ten-thousandths of
an inch long, but it has affected the economy, social
institutions, and even the religious complexion of the
continent.

During the mid-nineteenth century, Muslim Fulani
cavalry swept from their near-desert West African Sahel
kingdom into the savanna to the south and east, con-
quering and converting the animist tribes with whom
they came into contact. But in their progress through
woodlands and rain forests they encountered a formidable adversary, the tsetse. Swarms of these flies
attacked and bit the horses, transmitting the parasite to
them. It caused a lethal form of animal trypanosomiasis,
and in rapid order the cavalry became a disarrayed

infantry. On foot, the Fulani were virtually powerless; their invasion was halted before it could reach the great population centers of the Benue and Niger river valleys. Thus was Islam, with its concomitant sociopolitical influences, prevented from infiltrating this vast densely peopled region of Africa for more than half a century.

The popular notion of trypanosomiasis is represented by the image of a lethargic human suffering from the "sleeping distemper," to use the words of an English observer some two hundred years ago. Not a form of distemper at all, the infection is caused in man by one of two closely related parasitic organisms, *Trypanosoma gambiense* and *T. rhodesiense,* and in animals by *T. brucei, T. congolense,* and *T. vivax. (T. gambiense* was thought to be restricted to man, but researchers have recently implicated the pig as a reservoir host.) Both animal and human trypanosomes are transmitted by the tsetse, a bloodsucking fly of the genus *Glossina.* Tsetse flies inhabit Africa only south of the Sahara, from approximately fifteen degrees north to twenty degrees south latitude, although they once had wider distribution, as evidenced by the discovery of a fossilized tsetse in the Oligocene shales of Colorado. While human trypanosomiasis continues to be a public-health problem, being responsible for some seven thousand deaths each year, it is the infection in domestic animals that has had the greatest impact on African development.

The tsetse belt encompasses more than six million square miles of land denied to livestock production, mixed farming, and in some regions, human settlement. It is an area that could potentially provide 125 million head of cattle to the protein-starved continent. The disease has forced herdsmen to concentrate their stock on the limited amount of fly-free pasturage, and this practice has led to overgrazing and attendant soil erosion. When cattle are trekked to distant markets through fly-infested country, some 25 percent may die before reaching their destination. And yet, a less anthropocentric view might hold that by preventing overexploitation of this enormous area, the tsetse and the trypanosome are the most stalwart guardians of the African ecosystem and its magnificent wild fauna.

The manner and degree of transmission of trypanosomes involves complex interactions of parasite, host and fly vector. With this in mind, let us consider the scenario and dramatis personae of *The Fly That Would Be King*, an African spectacular with a cast of millions.

Act 1 is set in a forest in Africa. On stage is the host—a man, a cow, or an antelope. A closer, microscopic examination reveals the second character, the trypanosome, swimming about in the blood of the host by means of an undulating membrane and a lashing flagellum. A sound of angry buzzing comes from off stage. Enter a tsetse, a brown insect not much larger than a housefly. The tsetse smells and sights the host, then strikes and bites, sucking in its trypanosome-containing blood.

Act 2 takes place inside the tsetse's gut, where the trypanosome elongates and multiplies by simple asexual division. After about four days it migrates to the fly's salivary glands; there, over the next fifteen days, further transformation takes place, until it assumes the short, stumpy appearance of the metacyclic stage—the terminal developmental form, in which it is capable of infecting a new host.

Act 3 opens in the forest twenty days after act 1. The original host lies obviously ill on the stage floor. Enter another host. The infected tsetse strikes, delivering the metacyclic parasites to the blood stream of the new host and completing the cycle. Curtain.

While this plot is essentially the same for all African trypanosomes, the details for each species differ in important respects. In man, the disease caused by *T. gambiense* is chronic and malignant, and gives rise to the torpor and eventual coma and death classically associated with sleeping sickness.

The pathology of the disease is largely unknown. Over the course of time, the trypanosomes tend to leave the blood and enter, first, the lymphatics, and later, the spinal fluid and the tissues of the central nervous system. The patient becomes comatose during this latter phase, and dies after several years if he has not received chemotherapeutic treatment.

Whereas Gambian sleeping sickness results in a slow death, that caused by *T. rhodesiense* kills within weeks or months. The two infections differ not only in degree of virulence but in other respects as well. Gambian trypanosomiasis is essentially a human disease, cycled from person to person, while the transmission cycle of Rhodesian trypanosomiasis includes a third host—the wild antelope—which acts as a reservoir of infection. By all biological criteria, *T. rhodesiense* is a parasite of the wild ungulates, rather than man. Evolution has resulted in a state of equilibrium in which the parasite produces no overt disease in the animal host. Man, for the most part an accidental host, has not attained this accommodation, as the intense virulence of the human disease indicates. The manner by which the antelope modulates the infection remains a mystery; its elucidation might aid in devising a means of similarly stimulating a protective state in man.

The ecological setting—the landscape epidemiology—is different for each of these disease varieties. Gambian sleeping sickness is generally restricted to the humid forests bordering the lakes and rivers of West and Central Africa, the obligatory habitat of *G. palpalis*, the tsetse species that transmits this form of the disease.

Because rural African populations rarely have the means to obtain water from distant sources, communities tend to form along the banks of rivers and lakes, and village activities—bathing, washing, drawing water, and fishing—take place at the water's edge, making for intense man–fly contact. Epidemics flare from time to time, but generally the disease level is low because this tsetse is, biologically, a relatively inefficient vector. Trypanosomes can readily multiply in *G. palpalis* only shortly after the fly emerges from the pupal stage. Very few older flies are able to act as vectors after feeding upon infected humans.

Sleeping sickness caused by *Trypanosoma rhodesiense* is endemic to the dry savanna woodlands of East and Central Africa, the habitat of both the *G. morsitans* vector and the great herds of antelope that serve as reservoir hosts. Human infections occur when people settle in the savanna or intrude to hunt, gather wood, or graze cattle. The species of vector that transmits this form of the disease is not an equal-opportunity biter; and it prefers to take a blood meal from mammals other than humans. When game becomes scarce, however, the fly will feed on humans. Apparently attracted to large, slow-moving objects, it becomes confused when these sometimes turn out to be vehicles rather than antelope, and it will feed on the passengers. In this curious way, a package tour of East African game parks occasionally includes trypanosomiasis.

There is, then, an intimate relationship between the

nature of the ecosystem and the epidemiology of trypanosomiasis. The history of Africa, however, is characterized by continuous ecological change—with felled
rain forests succeeded by grasslands and savanna woodlands, an advancing or retreating desert, and shifting
distribution or concentration of human inhabitants and
wild fauna. These environmental changes have played
a crucial role in the epidemiological patterns of the
Gambian and Rhodesian forms of trypanosomiasis, particularly where their ranges overlap in east-central
Africa.

The activities and diseases of both Africans and colonial expatriates have also contributed to the epidemiological status of trypanosomiasis. Before the nineteenth-
century colonial period, trypanosomiasis was confined
to a relatively few smoldering foci. Internecine warfare
and lack of roads restricted communication and prevented the spread of the infection. The rapid dissemi-
nation of sleeping sickness can be traced to the opening
up of Africa by the colonial powers. It was the *Pax Bri-
tannica* as much as the tsetse that was responsible for the
broadcast of infection. How this complex of changing
environmental and human factors has influenced epi-
demicity of the two types of human trypanosomiasis is
illustrated, par excellence, by the events that have
occurred along the Kenya and Uganda shores of Lake
Victoria.

Prior to human settlement, the lake was surrounded
by a tropical high forest. Primitive farmers migrated to
the lake's shores and felled forest tracts for their shifting agriculture. Forest-inhabiting tsetse were present,
but human trypanosomiasis was absent. Eventually,
deforestation progressed to such a degree that grassland replaced large areas of forest. The grassland then

attracted a second wave of migration—Nilotic pastoralists (that is, herders who originated in the Nile basin) and Bantu cultivators. The combined pressures of grazing and agriculture suppressed forest regeneration and thus maintained a fly-free area beyond the forest that fringed the lake.

In the nineteenth century the society along the lake was devastated by the twin pestilences of smallpox and rinderpest, and agricultural activity diminished. Before the population had time to recover, savanna woodland succeeded the grassland. At the close of the nineteenth century the ecological stage was set for sleeping sickness. The shores of the lake were bordered by a rain forest infested with *G. palpalis,* the tsetse vector of *T. gambiense.* Beyond the forest *G. morsitans,* the vector of *T. rhodesiense,* inhabited the savanna woodland. Still the trypanosome had not made its debut.

The parasite is thought to have been introduced when Sir Henry Morton Stanley, employed at that time in the Congo by the Belgians, mounted an expedition in 1887 to the area of Lake Victoria. Natives in Stanley's retinue, probably infected with *T. gambiense,* may have carried the seeds of the epidemic that was to decimate the population for the next ten years.

By 1910, when the Gambian sleeping sickness began to burn itself out, the number of inhabitants in the area had declined from 300,000 to 100,000. Before the epidemic, the large size and number of human settlements had had the effect of suppressing the faunal population; but as people died of the disease or fled the stricken area, the game reservoirs of *T. rhodesiense* increased and moved into the adjacent savanna woodland. The final epidemiological link in the chain of Rhodesian sleeping sickness—from game to man through woodland-dwelling fly—was now present, to complete the cycle. When government-inspired resettlement was attempted in the 1940s, the migrants rapidly became infected with this highly lethal disease, and once again the inhabitants deserted the land. Today, this potentially rich region is virtually abandoned, occupied only by a few fishermen who are at high risk of contracting the infection.

When I joined the West African Institute for Trypanosomiasis Research in 1951, the entire infected population of Nigeria lay, so to speak, before me, but I was to be introduced to the human disease in a much more personal way and under circumstances that gave me a first glimpse into the meshing of the fly, the trypanosome, the ecosystem, and human behavior.

My friend Dan Quaddo, a Rukuba and in the epithets of that unregenerate colonial era, a pagan (being neither Christian nor Muslim) was the household "small boy" (the domestic of all work, age notwithstanding). He was a small, cheerful, but unbeautiful man; his name meant Son of the Frog, and West African "village" names are bestowed with deadly accuracy. The only maggot in Dan Quaddo's otherwise optimistic disposition was his unfathomable terror of "teef men" (pidgin for burglars, not dentists), and even during the hottest nights of the hot season he would barricade himself within his quarters. I once tried to reason with him: "Dan Quaddo, why do you do this? You are so poor and have so little, why would anyone want to teef you?" I vividly recall his reply, in which he explained with the patience of someone describing an immutable law to a small, rather dense child: "Suh, anyone who teef me be so bad he not need a reason."

A short time after this illuminating conversation he returned to his nearby village, on the slopes of the Bauchi Plateau, and spent several weeks there attending to "family affairs." A few weeks after returning he once again locked, bolted, and shuttered himself within his house, this time complaining not of "teef men," but of devils of fever and headache. The American reaction would be to exorcise these with aspirin, but in Africa, where malaria is commoner than the common cold, the first resort is routinely to the magic of antimalarial drugs. After a time the fever abated, but the headache persisted and Dan Quaddo became uncharacteristically eccentric and surly. He took to putting nonperishables in the refrigerator—theater tickets, tennis balls, my wife's brassière (the "small, small vest for chest"). There was no disputing that what ailed Dan Quaddo was not malaria and that he needed medical attention. In the tropics the microscopic examination of the blood takes pride of diagnostic precedence, and I remember peering into the microscope and seeing, for the first time outside a laboratory classroom, the trypanosomes of a human swimming in the microscopic field and the dancing movement of the red blood cells as they were disturbed by the thrashing parasites. We later found that Dan Quaddo's infection had progressed to the stage where his lymph glands had also been invaded by the Gambian trypanosomes, but fortunately the disease was caught before the central nervous system became involved. He was successfully treated and made an uneventful recovery. However, I was curious about how he had contracted the infection, since we were supposed to be outside the tsetse belt. Inquiry revealed that Dan Quaddo was actually one of the last victims of a cataclysmic sleeping-sickness epidemic, beginning some ten years earlier, that had brought his tribe to the verge of extinction.

In former times the outliers of the typical high forests

bordering streams and rivers had penetrated the dry savanna, and these outliers had provided a suitable ecological niche for the tsetse vector. The Rukubas had cut down most of the outliers, but each tribe preserved near its village a small area of forest that was sacred, the *tsafi* grove. The flies had retreated to these groves and were concentrated there in great numbers. Every seven years the elders and the young boys went to their sacred grove for a religious retreat, during which the youngsters were initiated into manhood. The secrets and mysteries of the Rukubas were passed from the old to the young, and the genealogy of the tribe was recounted. Circumcision rites were performed, and the elders harangued the initiates about morality. During these religious retreats man and fly were in close contact, but until the early 1940s the trypanosome was absent. The infection is believed to have originated with a farmer who, taking advantage of the relatively new state of intertribal tranquility imposed by the colonial government, traveled to the south of the plateau, an area of endemic trypanosomiasis. On his return, this farmer participated in a manhood initiation rite and was a source of infection to the fly and consequently to his coreligionists. The human infection slowly built in intensity, and by the mid-1940s one-fourth of some village populations had been stricken. When the first medical teams were sent to the area, the Rukubas either fled or hostilely ejected them from the villages. In 1944 they were finally convinced of their plight and accepted mass drug treatment and tsetse-eradication campaigns. By the early 1950s the epidemic, except for a trickle of infection, had been brought to a halt. My unfortunate friend Dan Quaddo, whose "family affairs" had really been a *tsafi*-grove ritual, was one of the last to become infected, and he had almost been "teefed" of his life. The trypanosome was indeed, so bad it didn't need a reason to rob him.

The trypanosomes that infect domestic animals are not restricted to any particular forest ecosystem; animal trypanosomiasis exists wherever there are tsetse flies of any species. The presence of wild-game reservoirs—along with the fact that the flies, in all probability, carry the trypanosomes (*T. brucei, T. congolense,* and *T. vivax*)—contributes to a level of transmission so intense and ubiquitous as to effectively preclude stock production in one-fourth of Africa. Nomadic and semisettled cattle-owning tribes have been forced to pasture their animals in the fly-free zones in and near the arid Sahel. As the dry season approaches, the Sahel is no longer able to sustain the herds and the annual trek into the fly-infested Guinea savanna begins. Losses to trypanosomiasis always occur, but where nutrition is adequate and the density of flies not too great, the stock may manage to survive, if not flourish.

The breed of cattle favored by the African pastoralist is the zebu, a large, humpbacked longhorn, well adapted to semiarid conditions. Although it produces relatively high yields of milk and meat, the zebu has the unfortunate disadvantage of being susceptible to trypanosomiasis. There are smaller, even dwarf, breeds of cattle, such as the N'dama and Muturu, that possess remarkably high resistance to or tolerance of the trypanosome. Studies carried out at the Nigerian Institute for Trypanosomiasis Research have proved that the resistance of these breeds is due to a highly efficient immune response. Two conditions are necessary for the attainment of this level of protective immunity. First, the animals must be born of a hyperimmune dam, and second, they must receive an early and continuous infection of trypanosomes, so that they produce a protective antibody.

These tolerant breeds have not as yet been economically exploited, probably because of their small size, although the N'dama is large enough to be used for meat. Crossbreeding with zebu or European breeds does not result in offspring capable of developing hyperimmunity.

Combating trypanosomiasis calls for heroic measures, but because of the severity of the side effects, the remedies may not be practicable. The battle against the disease has included massive alteration of the environment, social dislocation, wholesale slaughter of wild fauna, and the mass administration of toxic drugs. A commonly employed means of control has been to deny the tsetse its required habitat by selective or large-scale deforestation. Fly-free zones can only be maintained by intensive land use, brought about by the collectivization of the population into large agricultural villages and townships. This forced dislocation from the traditional, stable life in small, scattered tribal groups has resulted in a disturbing upheaval of the social order.

Perhaps the most controversial control measure was the game-destruction program carried out in East Africa during the 1950s. Designed to open up land to human settlement, this scheme was faultless in its logic. Game animals harbor *T. rhodesiense* and are the main source of blood for the tsetse; therefore, destroying the large fauna means good riddance to both trypanosome and fly. After the campaign, however, small mammals survived in sufficient numbers to support the fly population. Also, as the game was decimated, herdsmen moved their cattle into the cleared areas, the fly began to feed on the livestock and the pastoralists, and the result was continued and intensified transmission of both animal and human trypanosomes. Finally, revulsion against the studied slaughter brought the program to a halt.

Another possibility is to control the spread of the disease by means of insecticides. Ironically, one researcher, Dr. Walter Ormerod, has proposed that the use of insecticides was a major, if not prime, contributor to the great drought that recently ravaged sub-Saharan Africa. The reasoning of this hypothesis is as follows: Increasing urbanization and prosperity in West Africa precipitated a demand for meat. Traditional cattle-owning tribes increased the size of their herds to match the market. Widespread, government-sponsored aerial spraying of insecticides, in conjunction with mass chemoprophylactic injections of cattle, followed, permitting growth of herds not only in the Sahel but also in the adjacent Guinea savanna. The large numbers of cattle overgrazed the meager stands of grass and other plant life in this fragile ecosystem, resulting in a higher reflectance of sunlight from the denuded land. There is good evidence that such a situation causes a decrease in rainfall, and in this region matters did indeed proceed to a point where the result was climatic havoc.

Despite more than seventy years of research and effort, the freeing of Africa from trypanosomiasis has not been realized. The effective, practicable means of control now available are too harsh. Except for limited areas, insecticide spraying is too costly. Governments of the new African nations are often too poor in economic and technical resources to maintain the anti-trypanosome and anti-tsetse programs begun during the colonial era.

Drug treatment of infected people has brought about

a decline in human trypanosomiasis, but the trypanosomes can develop resistance. Confronted with this impasse, scientists have long sought the biological "magic bullet"—immunization—as a solution of the problem. Vaccination has brought many of the great scourges of mankind, such as smallpox and yellow fever, under control without necessitating changes in the environment or turmoil in the socioeconomic order. But unlike the immunologically amenable bacterial and viral pathogens, the trypanosome has confounded all attempts to induce protective immunity. The reason for this failure stems from the parasite's ability to elude the host's immune defense by a process known as antigenic variation.

There is currently great concern over the antigenic shift of the influenza virus, a phenomenon that seems to occur about every ten years. A trypanosome undergoes the same process, but a new antigenic variant arises every five to ten days. This is tantamount to the host's being assaulted by a new, personal epidemic each and every week.

During the course of a trypanosomal infection the host may develop an antibody that eliminates most, but not all, of the trypanosomes. The survivors are of a different antigenic character from the others, so the antibody fails to recognize them. The variant trypanosomes then begin to proliferate in the blood stream. The host responds by producing a new specific antibody. The process is repeated over and over, for the trypanosome possesses the remarkable ability of producing a large, probably infinite, number of antigenic variants.

The underlying mechanism responsible for antigenic variation has been the subject of a long controversy between those who hold it to be a selective process, which presupposes a starting parasite population of one predominant and many minor variants, and those who believe that antigenic variants arise by mutation. There are difficulties in supporting either of these explanations by experimental evidence. Electron microscopy and immunochemical analysis suggest that the trypanosome antigen—the face the parasite presents to its world—is a glycoprotein coat, or pellicle, situated outside the trypanosome's limiting plasma membrane. Apparently this coat is periodically shed, and the parasite, acting as its own couturier, designs and makes a new antigenic garment.

T. vivax, the important pathogen of livestock, seems to have developed still another maneuver to survive in the immunized host—antigenic mimicry. This trypanosome may be able to absorb a coat of host serum protein that disguises its alien status and also acts as a protective shield against any antibody that the host may produce. A similar phenomenon, the absorption of host substances to the external parasite surface, occurs in the schistosome blood flukes of man. Antigenic disguise may thus be another important adaptive evolutionary strategy that permits some parasites to exist in the immunized host.

New methods for dealing with human and animal trypanosomiasis are urgently needed. However, the extent of research and the amount of resources invested are minuscule compared to the magnitude of the problem. A new trypanocidal drug has not been added to the chemotherapeutic armamentarium for twenty years. Pharmaceutical companies candidly admit that the high cost of development and the potentially poor profits from selling to the generally impoverished underdeveloped nations have virtually taken them out of tropical-disease research. I feel confident, however, that improved means of combating the infections will eventually be forthcoming. A quality of biomedical science is its incurable optimism that all things are possible, given time and support.

But it may well be that Africa's real problems will commence with the effective control of trypanosomiasis. Scientists and the administrators carrying out the practical applications of research often fail to recognize that they are engaged in a gigantic chess game. As one enemy piece is captured, other pieces move to threaten. As trypanosomiasis is conquered, overgrazing, soil erosion, social disruption, and faunal extinction may result. Until the time comes when scientists and their technical-administrative partners appreciate the grand strategy of acting sanely and effectively to protect the well-being of all Africa's citizens, both two-legged and four-legged, we may applaud the cosmic wisdom that has made the tsetse, rather than man, Africa's custodian.

7

RIVER BLINDNESS

Information has reached me that the village of St. Pierre has disappeared; all that is known of it is that the houses are completely deserted and broken down.

—A. Rolland, 1972

In 1963 a small band of settlers, driven by hunger, left their overpopulated and infertile land in the savanna of West Africa and migrated to the banks of the Keralie River, a tributary of the Black Volta. There, they built the village of Saint Pierre and began to farm the rich valley land.

Five years later, 75 percent of these pioneers had developed ocular lesions. Some were already functionally blind. Finally, life and sight became too precarious and they fled. By the time epidemiologist A. Rolland made his report, Saint Pierre had become one more ghost town of the West African savanna—another community crumbled by the parasitic filarial worm *Onchocerca volvulus* and its vector, the blackfly *Simulium damnosum.*

The disease onchocerciasis, familiarly known in Africa as river blindness, has a quality of gothic horror not shared by other tropical infections. Malaria decimates the young but usually leaves the survivors sufficiently immune to be productive members of their community. Trypanosomiasis denies vast areas of Africa the benefits of mixed farming and the protein that could be provided by domestic animals, but basic agriculture is rarely disrupted, and except for sporadic outbreaks, the prevalence of human sleeping sickness is now low. Onchocerciasis, in contrast, dispossesses people from the most fertile agricultural land and blinds those who would dare tenant its dominion.

The victims are rural peasants, too often neglected by the political, medical, and technological panjandrums concentrated in the great cities. Therapy by the few effective drugs available can be worse than the disease. Control of the blackfly vector is so costly and demanding that it is beyond the capabilities of most of the affected Third World nations. The disease afflicts at least fifty million people; yet since it doesn't kill, only a handful of scientists have undertaken research on how to combat the parasite and its vector.

The major center of onchocerciasis is in West Africa, but pockets of infection also exist in East Africa and Yemen, and in the New World from Mexico to Brazil. Infected West African slaves, met on arrival by indigenous species of blackfly, probably introduced the disease into the Americas. As early as 1590, more than a thousand slaves were imported annually from endemic areas of West Africa to work the placer gold-mining operations in Colombia and Venezuela. The fast-flowing streams carrying gold were also ideal breeding habitats for the blackfly, and the infection, established almost four hundred years ago, persists in these remote areas.

Not the slave trade, but a French military adventure was responsible for the importation of the disease into Mexico. In 1862, Napoleon III sent Sudanese troops to Oaxaca to assist the French invasion forces. These Sudanese came from an area where onchocerciasis was—and is—prevalent, and according to Mexican historians, signs of infection turned up not long after the troops arrived. Foci of disease exist today in the Mexican and Guatemalan highlands at an altitude of 1,600 to 5,000 feet, where the main blackfly vector, *Simulium ochracaeum*, breeds in the mountain streams. This is also the altitude where the coffee plantations are situated, and the bitterness of that epidemiological brew is that 30 to 75 percent of the plantation workers are infected with the parasite. The current cost of some of our favorite "mountain-grown" coffee is indeed high, not only in dollars per pound but also in atrophied skin, itching eruptions, eye disorders, and blindness.

The filarial nematode that causes river blindness is a first cousin to the filaria parasites that produce the notorious elephantiasis, with its grotesque disfigurements of limbs and genitalia. The adult worms are threadlike creatures that live encapsulated within fibrous nodules beneath the human skin. The eggs, like those of all filarial worms, hatch within the uterus of the female worm. Each female worm can give birth to two thousand or more of the microscopic, snakelike larvae, the microfilariae, every day of the fifteen to twenty years of her life within a human. Upon leaving the mother, the microfilariae disperse to the upper layers of the skin and to other parts of the body, including the eye.

The next act in the biological scenario takes place when the biting blackfly ingests microfilariae. Within the blackfly, the parasite passes through a series of transformations, first in the gut, then in the muscles of the thorax. After a final metamorphosis into a slender, filariform larva (the infective stage), it migrates to the head and mouth parts. This cycle takes about two weeks. The filariform larvae escape when the blackfly bites a human; they enter the subcutaneous tissues, grow to adulthood, and mate. About nine months later the females begin producing the microfilariae.

When I was what now seems a very young junior officer in the Nigerian Colonial Medical Research Service, I used to spend my local leaves fishing on the Gurara and Benue rivers for the tiger fish, that splendid warrior of the African rivers, and for the "elephant of the waters," the Niger perch. I recall wondering—with the innocence and narrow interest of youth (I was "into" sleeping sickness in those days)—why so many of the local men who accompanied us on those trips looked so old. It seemed cruel of the chiefs to send these ancients to bear our loads.

I realize now that most of these "ancients" were probably not much older than I and had been propelled into premature senility by the *Onchocerca* microfilariae in their skin. Some fifty years ago, a physician working in the Sudan commented that "onchocerciasis makes young people look old and old people look like lizards."

The microfilariae cause a chronic inflammation of the skin tissues, accompanied by an itching so intense that some of the afflicted have been driven to suicide. In time, the normal architecture of the skin vanishes, replaced by a toneless, thickened, depigmented covering—the pachyderm skin. The skin over the groin may become so loose as to hang down like a kind of bizarre apron. The lesions in the eye, however, produce the most serious consequences of onchocerciasis. As the microfilariae invade the cornea, the anterior chamber, the retina, and even the optic nerve, the mechanical damage and inflammatory response of the immunologically "outraged" host can lead to partial loss of sight and, eventually, total blindness.

The clinical end products of the infection have been well characterized, but the mechanisms underlying their pathogenesis are dimly understood. They apparently involve the human immune system. The level of functional immunity is relatively low despite high levels of antibody production. The host's cellular reaction to the dying microfilaria is more severe than to the living one (possibly, like some other parasites, the living microfilaria masquerades, antigenically, as a human). We have a glimmer that in the worst cases part of the immune system may de depressed, and this has led to the suggestion that the pathological "entity" may be a conjugate of the human antibody and the antigen released by the dying worm.

One reason why we have little more than glimmers, suggestions, and hypotheses concerning pathogenesis and immunity is that we lack a satisfactory experimental model. The parasitic worm is steadfastly devoted to its human host and refuses to infect any conventional laboratory animal. Humans in endemic areas are generally inaccessible and naturally cannot, and should not, be manipulated for experimental purposes. A related species of nematode, *Onchocerca gutturosa*, infects cattle. The pathological picture differs from that in man, however, and at any rate, the cow is not exactly the most available animal for laboratory-based scientists, especially those working within the limitations of current research budgets.

Different ecosystems have sibling species of different

character, of both the parasite and the blackfly vector. For the biologist, observing the fascinating variations among these sibling species is like being a spectator at a game of evolution played out on a gigantic scale. For the clinician and epidemiologist, this incipient speciation has considerable practical importance.

Variations in the clinical expression of infection in humans raised the first suspicions that the parasites of the humid forest and those of the savanna might be different, despite their identical morphology. Infection rates are generally very high among forest dwellers, in many instances higher than among people living in savanna communities, yet severe optic pathology is unusual among them. One study showed that in forest people the rate of eye disease was 4 percent, while in the savanna village examined it was 34 percent, despite similar over-all infection rates for the two groups. Infected forest people do not escape unaffected; the other manifestations, such as skin lesions and thickening, are all there.

Two English workers, B. O. L. Duke and J. Anderson, have provided a degree of experimental confirmation that the forest and savanna parasites differ in their virulence. Microfilariae obtained from savanna patients were more invasive and produced more severe optic lesions in rabbits than did microfilariae obtained from forest patients. (The microfilariae will live for a time in abnormal hosts, though the adult worms will not.) More recently, another English group, led by Anthony Bryceson, found distinct differences in antigenic composition between parasites of the forest and those of the savanna.

The major African blackfly vector, *S. damnosum,* has also evolved in separate directions in the forest and in the savanna. Again, behavioral differences were the first clues to incipient speciation. For example, the smell of humans is what primarily attracts the forest blackfly, while the sight of humans, rather than odor, impels the savanna blackfly to feed. By classic morphological criteria, all *S. damnosum* are identical, but an elegant new technique, cytotaxonomy, has revealed that, in fact, this blackfly has evolved into a complex of species. An examination of the giant polytene chromosomes* in the salivary glands—by experts who can read their distinctive pattern of bands like a road map—has shown that forest and savanna blackflies are two separate species. This speciation of both parasite and vector within the two ecosystems has also led to a lack of reciprocity in vector–parasite relationships. When blackflies captured in the forest are fed on onchocerciasis patients from the savanna, no infection develops in the blackfly. Nearly all the microfilariae are rapidly destroyed while still inside the blackfly's gut.

For the human voyager, "getting there" may be half the fun if one can believe the blandishments of the travel industry, but for the vector-borne parasite, getting there is essential to survival. The habitat and behavior of the vector largely determine if the parasite will successfully make the crucial journey from host to host. In common with most insect vectors, blackflies are highly selective in their choice of breeding habitat; this selectivity is fundamental to the epidemiology of onchocerciasis.

---

*Polytene chromosomes, which are found in the nucleus of the cells in certain insect tissues, are "giant" in size. When appropriately stained they display a coded banding characteristic for the insect's genetic type—somewhat analogous to the characteristic spectrum band of an inorganic element. Analysis of the polytene-chromosome bands can make possible the taxonomic identification of closely related insect species that may in other respects be morphologically indistinguishable.

The female blackfly deposits her eggs only in fast-flowing, well-oxygenated water containing sufficient organic debris to nourish the filter-feeding larvae. (They consume particulate organic matter filtered out of the water by brushlike appendages on the mouth.) The larvae attach themselves to stones, aquatic vegetation, or the limbs of trees dipping into the water (one East African species has developed the curious habit of attaching to the backs of fresh-water crabs). From these breeding sites, the emergent adult blackflies disperse for many miles into the surrounding bush, where they make a formidable barrier, denying the fertile river valley to human settlement and agriculture. In endemic areas, infection rates begin to decline only beyond a distance of as much as ten miles from the river.

Unfortunately, human attempts to exploit the riverine land often initiate a tragic cycle. Before human settlement, the rivers and streams usually run clear, providing insufficient suspended organic matter to maintain a large population of blackfly larvae. Where the density of adult blackflies is low, the human population increases through normal growth, and immigration into the sparsely inhabited riverine bush occurs. Land use intensifies deforestation. In these highly cultivated watersheds, the soil erodes and the land loses its ability to hold rainfall. River courses and flow patterns change. During the wet seasons, the once clear rivers carry enormous amounts of suspended organic matter—providing ideal conditions for the prolific breeding of blackflies.

Biting increases to such a degree that each person may receive fifty thousand infective-stage larvae each year. The attack of the flies is itself almost unbearable (readers who have suffered blackfly bites while flogging our northern trout streams can sympathize with the plight of the African). Finally, the onset of eye lesions destroys the community. In time the people abandon the village and retreat to the arid savanna or the equally arid fly-free highlands. There they rapidly deplete the soil in a futile attempt to feed themselves. Starvation drives them back to the river, and generation after generation they yo-yo between hunger and blindness.

Grandiose hydroelectric schemes have had both beneficial and harmful effects on onchocercal endemicity. To be charitable to the master builders, the lakes they have created behind the damns have obliterated stretches of river where blackflies formerly bred. The huge, man-made Lake Volta in Ghana relieved an area two hundred miles long of the fly. (Unfortunately, charity must end with onchocerciasis. Creation of this same lake brought a marvelous four-thousand-mile shoreline to attract the blood fluke *Schistosoma haematobium,* and as the lake filled, the prevalence of this parasite in the schoolchildren of some lakeside villages soared from 1 percent to 100 percent.)

Below the dams, the transmission of river blindness has often intensified. The kilowatts that lit the cites have extinguished the light for thousands of rural inhabitants. The largest dams, with the largest lakes—such as the Volta scheme—have a constant flow of water over the spillways. Not only does the blackfly breed in the courses below the spillways, but the continuous water flow permits perennial breeding and causes perennial transmission of the disease. The natural cessation of the river's flow in the dry season, which once brought about a drastic diminution of the vector population, no longer occurs.

The remedy for onchocerciasis may perpetuate ecological imbalance. The obvious solution to the problem is to eliminate either the vector or the parasite. The main effort has been to reduce blackfly breeding to a level where little or no transmission occurs. Alarmed by the havoc of onchocerciasis in the Volta River basin, an international consortium led by the World Health Organization, and bankrolled by the United Nations Development Program to the tune of $120 million over a twenty-year period, is trying to do just that.

The method of control has been to apply DDT and other insecticides to the breeding waters. However, the parasite is long-lived in humans, surviving for fifteen to twenty years, so to eradicate the infection by this strategy requires that insecticides be infused into the water for up to twenty years, until all the microfilaria carriers become "burnt-out" cases. The insecticides kill not only the blackfly larvae but also their natural predators. If control measures are halted prematurely, unrestrained recolonization may occur, followed by even more intensified transmission. This has, in fact, happened at least once, on the Ivory Coast.

The option of mass drug administration against the parasite is also foreclosed because the sole microfilaricidal agent available, diethylcarbamazine (DEC), causes adverse reactions so severe as to preclude its use except under careful medical supervision. DEC, which is produced under the name Hetrazan, is the workhorse of antifilarial compounds. Although it has been used for forty years, virtually nothing is known about how it acts on the parasite. One can take microfilariae, put them in a test tube containing a solution of DEC at high concentration, and watch them continue to wiggle about in lively fashion. Yet the microfilariae die quickly in the treated patient.

The current theory holds that the drug changes the parasite in some unknown way to allow the host's immune system to destroy it. Whatever its mode of action, DEC is effective. It is also cheap. It is also damnably toxic, and the reason for this too has remained an unsolved mystery. DEC is perfectly safe and nontoxic when given to an uninfected person. When an individual with filariasis takes the drug, however, an adverse reaction develops, ranging in severity from headache and fever to death from a shocklike syndrome of the sort that can be triggered by allergy. DEC treatment of the other forms of filariasis, such as the Bancroftian and Malayan lymphatic types, rarely produces severe adverse reactions. But in posttreatment reactions of onchocerciasis patients, an itchy rash will occur, accompanied by a fall in blood pressure and occasionally by the collapse of the patient. While the symptoms may seem like those caused by a bee sting in a hypersensitive individual, the reaction is not a typically allergic one in that antihistamines fail to block it.

My colleagues and I, intrigued by this phenomenon, have been experimentally chipping away for the past several years in an effort to understand the underlying cause of the reaction and to acquire a means to prevent it. We have used, as a model, the only form of animal filariasis in which DEC may initiate a side reaction so untoward as to be fatal—dog heartworm (*Dirofilaria immitis*). So far we have only bits and pieces of small, tantalizing insights. When the infected dog becomes distressed an hour or two after being given DEC, one class of the antibodies in its blood disappears almost completely. In some dogs the IgE "allergic" antibody goes, while in others the IgG precipitating antibody disappears. The dog's temperature rises, its blood pressure falls, the liver is adversely affected, and the number of platelets (those small, round cells in the blood intimately involved in coagulation) plummets. The substance or substances responsible for this pathological cascade have defied isolation so far.

One hypothesis is that the reaction somehow arises from the union of antibody with the worm antigen. A blackboard in my laboratory has lists of all the findings and arrows that show the possible pathways and relationships. From time to time a graduate student or visitor will contemplate this *Gemisch* of data and draw in another line. The blackboard has begun to look like a Jackson Pollock painting. Meanwhile we are experimenting empirically with known blocking agents that act on certain pathways, hoping that chance will favor our prepared minds. We are not even certain that the events occurring in the dog also occur in the treated human. But at least we have some idea of what to look for when we move from the laboratory to field and stream.

In one of his more enlightened manifestoes, Lenin once exhorted, "Devastate the worms!" But the revolution, in the form of more effective and safer drugs and larvicides, is yet to come for the tropical proletariat under the yoke of onchocerciasis. Until that jubilee day, means will have to be found to implement the measures now available, and the planners of great schemes will have to adopt the physician's guiding principle: first do no harm.

8

CONTROLLING THE SCHISTOSOME AT A SNAIL'S PACE

There is a hilarious episode in the movie *The Apprenticeship of Duddy Kravitz* that makes a sly comparison of the rituals of savage and sophisticate. Duddy, a young entrepreneur with a surfeit of chutzpah, is engaged in the business of filming the weddings, bar mitzvahs, and suchlike events that punctuate our lives. As the scene opens, Duddy and his director, a man slightly unhinged, are screening their latest epic. It shows a bar mitzvah. Present at the screening are the beaming parents, the boy who recently became a fully fledged member of Judaism's fraternity, and the rabbi who officiated at the event. Duddy's movie begins in an orthodox enough fashion, with the boy intoning the portion of the Torah, and then, with surgical suddenness cuts into a scene of a pagan rite. Savages. Wild men screaming and carrying on in demonic fashion. Then a cut back to the serenity of the bar mitzvah, and then back to the pagans—the shifting ritualistic counterpoint continuing until the end of the film. The lights go on, and we see the stunned parents looking to the rabbi for judgment of this unexpected offering. The rabbi, after thinking for a moment—perhaps seeking guidance from the Higher Critic—pronounces it to be an avant-garde milestone in the art of bar mitzvah films, and the tension eases visibly.

The scene stuck, with nagging persistence, in my thoughts. Upon later reflection I decided that this was because during my years in Africa and Asia I had perceived a commonality in all ritualistic celebration, whether by the tribe of Israel or the tribe of Ibo. I think this commonality is particularly shared by the rituals that mark the coming of age—that beautifully magic formal moment when a society recognizes the signs of passage from childhood to the obligations of adulthood. But in Africa there is one frightful marker of impending sexual and social maturity that is blessedly absent in the temperate world; at puberty the urine of the African youth may turn red with blood. This is so common an occurrence that in many parts of Africa it is considered to be a kind of male menstruation. The offender, in fact, is a parasitic worm living within the veins surrounding the bladder, whose clinical expression usually begins, for reasons not fully understood, during the early teens of the infected host. This blood fluke, *Schistosoma haematobium,* and the two other species commonly infecting humans, *S. mansoni* and *S. japonicum,* impose a burden of debility in the tropics second only to that resulting from malaria. The infection is water-associated, transmitted by fresh-water snails, and it is essentially a disease that humans bring upon themselves: it is now increasing in range and intensity as a result of agricultural and water-impoundment projects.

Like malaria and other infectious diseases, schistosomiasis has played a role in human history, and at least
once in our generation it influenced the political destiny
of a region.

In 1948 the Nationalist armies of Chiang Kai-shek,
having met defeat at the hands of the Communists, fled,
along with thousands of civilians of similar political persuasion, to refuge in Taiwan. It was a chaotic moment,
marked by political and military uncertainty. The
American ship of state had not yet sailed to protect
these troubled waters, and the Communists intended to
consolidate their victory by taking Taiwan. They rushed
some 200,000 troops from northern China to encamp-
ments along the lower Yangtze River to train for an
amphibious assault.

One hundred years before, in 1847, the physician
Dariji Fujii journeyed to the Lacquer Mountain, Katayama, in the Hiroshima prefecture of Japan. Dr. Fujii
was the first to describe the affliction of the local people
during the rice-planting season. The first sign, which
appears after the victim had waded in the rice paddies,
was a relatively innocent rash of the legs. Not long after,
the disease announced itself with fever and bloody diarrhea. Some of those affected continued to waste away,
and died. Dr. Fujii noted in his diary that to his frustra-
tion the medicines for "boosting spirits," for the "four-
times-rebellious disease," and for "poisoned people"
were of no avail. The cause of Katayama disease was to
remain a mystery for another sixty years, until another
physician, Katsurada, proved its symptoms to be the
early manifestations of S. japonicum infection.

This set of symptoms, still known today as Katayama
disease, struck the Communist troops. Northern China,
where these troops originated, is schistosome-free, but

the lower Yangtze River was at that time one of the most massively and intensely endemic areas of japonicum schistosomiasis. Within weeks of their arrival the men were paralyzed with fever and diarrhea. Some came running, but few went marching. An assault by troops so weakened by illness was out of the question, and the invasion was postponed. During that respite, American policy solidified. Taiwan became our protégé. Our navy steamed offshore. We had made the commitment to Asia.

But what would have happened if the schistosome had not been in the Yangtze Valley or the Communist troops had not fallen to the sickness of the Lacquer Mountain? Would the United States have turned its back on the East and ceded to the Chinese their traditional suzerainity? Would we have become involved in Vietnam? Would our present entente with the People's Republic of China have come to be, or would it have come about even earlier? We shall, of course, never know, but I strongly suspect that scholars would be writing a different history of Asia and America if not for the primitive flatworm.

The mantle of schistosomiasis is enormous. However, S. japonicum, which for countless centuries was highly endemic in Asia, has now receded, largely as a result of a herculean control effort by the Chinese and of the destruction by the Japanese of snail-breeding sites (some of the most important former habitats are now housing estates, factories, and golf courses). Intense foci of japonicum schistosomiasis still exist in some islands of the Philippines and in the Celebes, in Indonesia. A parasite resembling S. japonicum has recently been discovered infecting humans living along the Mekong River in Laos, where it is, as far as we can tell, localized. There is, however, concern that if the Mekong River project is ever completed, new habitats for the snail host will be created and the infection will be disseminated along extensive stretches of the river.

S. *mansoni* is highly prevalent in Africa, extending from the Nile Delta south through the greater part of the continent below the Sahara. And Mansonian schistosomiasis is also entrenched in Latin America, having been introduced, as if for revenge, by African slaves. It was tropical America's bad luck and the schistosome's good fortune that suitable snail hosts were awaiting the arrival of these slaves. Today, schistosomiasis is a major, unresolved health problem in Brazil, Venezuela, Surinam, and many Caribbean islands, including Puerto Rico.

In Africa, S. *haematobium* covers much of the same geographic range as S. *mansoni*. It is also present in the Middle East (in Iraq, Syria, Saudi Arabia, and Iran). Until it was eradicated about a decade ago by ecological measures and treatment of infected individuals, there was a small focus of urinary schistosomiasis along Israel's Yarkon River, perpetuated by orthodox (and infected) oriental Jewish women who took their ritual *mikveh* bath in the river and its tributaries.

That is the where of the schistosome. The why of the parasite is rooted in the complexities of its life cycle. And a complex life cycle it is—a marvel of development but a plague to student and reader (to whom apologies are made on behalf of author and schistosome). But in the Great Worm War we must ferret out the most subtle and secret facts of our enemy's life, so as to devise an effective battle plan. Knowledge of the developmental cycle allows our scientific counter intelligence corps to discern the weaker links in the transmission chain.

Understanding of the parasite's chemical physiology provides (theoretically at least) a means of developing effective chemical and pharmaceutical weapons. If we know the mechanisms underlying the immuno-pathological process we may be able to prevent infection and disease by modulating the human host's natural defenses. Also from this intelligence base, we may be able to anticipate the kind of blunders by our own political and technological high command that would cede the advantage to the parasite. So for these reasons let us examine the lives and loves of the schistosome.

The schistosome is an uxorious worm. The relatively stout cylindrical male, three-quarters of an inch long, has a grooved canal along the length of its underside. In this canal the female lies in constant embrace; they are monogamous and mated for life, which may be as long as thirty years. The worm's homestead is within a vein, where it is fixed to the vessel wall by means of two holdfast suckers at its anterior end. Each species of schistosome has adopted a venue in a particular compartment of the venous system; S. mansoni lives in the veins draining the lower intestine, S. japonicum in the veins of the upper intestine, and S. haematobium in the network of veins surrounding the bladder.

The female is a superefficient reproductive machine, daily producing approximately 3,500 eggs, each containing a fully formed larva, the miracidium. To continue the life cycle the egg must pass first through the wall of the vein and then through the wall of the bladder or bowel. How the egg broaches these formidable barriers is still uncertain. It is equipped with a spine, which evidently helps catch it on the vein's lining and protects it from being swept away by the circulating blood. Electron microscopy reveals that the egg has many minute pores, like a sieve, and the miracidium is believed to secrete a digestive enzyme that passes through these pores to the tissues and acts as a kind of meat tenderizer to facilitate passage. Only about 30 percent of the eggs make it to the lumen of the bowel or bladder, to be voided with feces or urine. Some eggs remain entrapped within the wall of the vein, or of the intestine or bladder, while some are carried by the blood stream to other organs, notably the liver, where they are filtered out into the surrounding tissues. As we shall see, it is the eggs that remain in the tissues that are the primary exciting agents of acute disease.

Shortly after the egg reaches the water, it hatches; the miracidium is released. The body of the larva is covered with "rowing hairs," the cilia, and for a brief period it lives free in the vastness of its water environment. But it must find a snail host within twenty-four hours or die. It was once believed that the miracidium came to the snail only by chance, but recent research has shown that there is a guidance system. The snail's "body odor"— emitted by a secretion of amino acids, fatty lipids, and possibly certain metallic ions—acts as a powerful attractant. Homing in on this chemical beam, the miracidium contacts the snail and by means of enzymatic secretions and vigorous drilling movement penetrates the snail's foot or antenna and migrates to the innards.

While this system helps the miracidium locate potential snails, it is not highly refined, and the secretions from suitable and unsuitable species of snail are equally attractive. But the schistosome's requirements for a host, like those of most vector-borne parasites, are very specific. *S. mansoni* will develop in *Biomphalaria* snails but not in species of *Bulinus,* while *S. haematobium* develops in *Bulinus* but *Biomphalaria* is refractory. Even more exacting limitations exist; over their broad geographic range, schistosomes and their snail hosts have evolved to a degree of narrow interdependence. For example, the species of genus *Bulinus* that is the vector of *S. haematobium* in Egypt cannot be infected with the West African strain of that parasite. It is even possible, by careful selective breeding in the laboratory, to isolate from a normally susceptible species of snail a subpopulation that will be resistant to infection. Susceptibility and resistance appear to be controlled by only one or two genes, but what chemicophysiological determinants are programmed by these genes is a secret that scientists have not yet been able to unlock.

However, let us return to our lucky miracidium, which has found and entered a compatible snail. I think what has always attracted me to animal parasites (fortunately the attraction hasn't been mutual; only on one occasion have they been attracted to me) is their remarkable, almost magical ability to transform, like Nature's Merlins, anatomically, functionally, physiologically, and antigenically as they proceed through their life cycle. It is as if they become entirely different creatures at each stage of development. In keeping with this phenomenon, the free-living miracidium transforms within the snail into an elongated sac, the mother sporocyst, whose sole function is asexual reproduction. The wall of this sac is lined with germinal cells that give rise to miniature replicas of itself. These daughter sporocysts grow and in turn reproduce—not other sporocysts, but the infective stage of the parasite, the tadpolelike, forked-tailed cercaria. This proliferation is staggeringly prodigious; as many as 250,000 cercariae will result from a single miracidium.

The cercariae leave the snail in daily waves, usually

between 8 A.M. and noon. Again, time is a critical factor for survival, for each cercaria must find its final host within two to three days. Enter (into the water) the fisherman, the housewife doing the family wash, the bathing child, the rice farmer, or your author, who has gone to retrieve a pygmy goose for dinner, and contact is made. The cercaria can also meet its host in drinking water. Upon contacting the mucous membrane or skin it flicks off its tail and penetrates, aided by enzymatic secretions from specialized glands. It rests from its labor for a day or so in the skin tissue, and during that time transforms into a juvenile worm, the schistosomula. Then it gets its migrational motor in gear and enters a small blood vessel, which carries it to the liver by way of the heart and lungs. It pauses for a mandatory sojourn in the liver, where it grows into a sexually mature female or male adult. Then this blind, unthinking worm migrates, with the certainty of a traveler holding a confirmed booking, to the venous compartment for which it is, as a species, destined. In the veins, boy schistosome meets girl schistosome, but how this liaison is brought about is not fully understood. There is now some evidence that parasitic worms secrete a powerful aphrodisiac, possibly similar to the pheromones of insects, that may guide the schistosomes to their sanguine tryst. One to three months after the cercariae have made that fateful meeting with their host—the exact time varies with the species—the female schistosome's genital assembly line begins cranking out her daily quota of eggs.

Let us review the stages of the life cycle, observing how they cause disease. Trouble for the host can begin with the pinhead-sized cercaria's penetration of the skin. The parasite's proteolytic secretions may cause a transient rash. With repeated exposure many individuals become sensitized and cercarial penetration incites an intense itching, accompanied by blister formation. Actually, cercarial dermatitis is not confined to the tropics; it has been a bothersome plague to bathers and other human aquatic waders in many parts of the world. Numerous animals, including water birds, have "their" species of schistosome. The cercariae of these animal parasites will penetrate the skin of the human, although they can mature no further in that abnormal host. In some places, bird schistosomes can cause reactions as intense as those produced by the human-schistosome cercariae. The description given by a man inflamed with cercarial dermatitis after bathing in a lake near Seattle is typical: "While drying myself with a towel I noticed that my skin turned red, and in a few minutes my arms and legs burned as though on fire."

Once the cercaria is under the skin it transforms into a schistosomula. This stage excites no pathological reaction. In fact, the schistosomula is the stage most vulnerable to the host's immune defenses. In an "immunological virgin," such as a tourist or young child, the schistosomula migrates and matures more or less unmolested. But in an experienced, immunologically primed host, the slaughter of most of the schistosomulae is accomplished by a complex co-operation of antibody and of specialized cells. Antibody and a serum protein "binder" (complement) coat the surface of the schistosomula. Certain cells, a subpopulation of lymphocytes and mast cells, send out a chemically signaled call for help to another type of white blood cell, the eosinophil. Eosinophils swarm to the scene and bind to the antibody which is bound to the parasite. The eosinophils, now blanketing the schistosomula, give the parasite the kiss of death by discharging a toxic substance into it. A few of the parasites escape; why they should be so privileged is not known.

The adult worm and the schistosomula share a number of antigens in common, and it struck researchers that, unaccountably, the immune response stimulated by these antigens killed the young schistosomulae but left the adults completely unaffected. The mystery was solved several years ago when it was discovered that the schistosome is yet another parasitic artful dodger masquerading as a human being. The developing schistosomes acquire host red-blood-cell and certain serum protein antigens on their surface. So when the immunized host's antibody molecules and killer cells come in search of the alien parasite, the schistosome responds, in effect, "There ain't nobody here but us humans."

There is little, or no, host reaction to the adult worm. The parasite isn't killed, but it doesn't excite an inflammatory response. It is the eggs, not disguised by host antigens, to which the host responds vigorously, and these are the chief cause of pathogenicity. You will remember that more than half the eggs become entrapped within the tissues. The antigens, the excreted products of the living miracidium within each egg, are what cause the host to react and overreact. Masses of immunocompetent cells—specialized white blood cells and nomadic macrophages—are mobilized, and surround each egg. Dr. David Wyler, of the National Institutes of Health, has shown that the egg antigens also call forth, and induce proliferation of, fibrocyte cells. In time, the egg becomes encapsulated in a thick coat of fibrous material. The immune system at this time is as hyperactive as the broom of the Sorcerer's Apprentice; it doesn't switch off after its mission has been accomplished. The mass of fibrous reactive tissue about the egg gets bigger and bigger, replacing the host's normal tissue. The heavier the infection, the more numerous the eggs and the greater the loss of organ tissue. In infection by *S. haematobium* there is early bleeding (the source of the blood in the young men's "menstrual" urine) as the eggs break through the ulcerated bladder wall. As the inflammatory response proceeds, the bladder loses its muscularity, becoming thickened and toneless. Urination in these advanced cases is painful and difficult.

While the pathological changes in the bladder and intestinal wall are undoubtedly serious, the most debilitating effects stem from the *S. mansoni* and *S. japonicum* eggs that are carried to the liver, where they are filtered out into the tissues surrounding the small veins. The egg-induced fibrosis surrounding these vessels can become so extensive that if the liver were cut open it would appear to be transected by a mass of thick white pipes. In fact, pathologists refer to this condition as clay-pipestem cirrhosis. These perivascular collars narrow the vein, and blood flow is impeded. The body's pipes are blocked, and its fluid, the blood, produces a back pressure—portal hypertension. The blood itself also backs up, through the venous connection, and the spleen becomes engorged and enlarged. The lungs may be similarly affected. When the pulmonary blood vessels are obstructed, the burden of the back pressure falls on the heart's right ventricle. The heart makes an effort to compensate, but if the condition is not ameliorated it can be fatal.

If this train of pathological events were to continue, many, if not most, of those infected would ultimately die. Fortunately, the immune system has a regulatory component that dispatches another group of specialized white blood cells, the suppressor cells, which emit chemical signals to switch off the process. Certain antibodies probably also act as a modulating feedback mechanism. But for some it is already too late when the immune system decides "enough, already," and these individuals either die or remain seriously disabled. *S. japonicum* is particularly virulent, not only because of the high fecundity of the female, but also because the suppressor arm of the immune system seems immobilized in infections with this species. There is also some evidence that for some unknown reason people with blood of group A are more likely to develop severe hepatosplenic schistosomiasis than are infected individuals of other blood groups. Factors such as malnutrition and the presence of other infections also enhance the schistosome's pathogenicity. And always, the children and young adults suffer most.

The "compensated" cases survive and are fit enough to carry on, meeting their modest personal needs. But even in this large group, the parasites exact their subtle toll in human energy. It has, for example, been variously estimated that Egypt loses somewhere between 4 percent and 35 percent of its productivity to the schistosome. The parasite robs each infected Filipino of an estimated $50 to $100 each year, no small amount considering the meager average annual income of the peasant. In a Tanzanian sugar estate where a bonus for extra work was used to measure the effect of antischistosomal chemotherapy on productivity, it was reckoned, at the end of the study, that out of a total labor force of 1,700, the schistosome was in effect deducting 38 laborers.

Water, poverty, and unsanitary habits are the basic ingredients for schistosomal endemicity. The poor of the tropics will be with us, if not forever, at least for the foreseeable future. Their unsanitary customs are unlikely to change until their economic fortunes improve. But while poverty and habit have perpetuated the infection, they have played only a small part in its intensification. It is the manipulation of tropical water resources, ostensibly for the national good, that is responsible for the spread and increased prevalence of schistosomiasis today. That schistosomiasis will be a consequence of any tropical water-impoundment project constructed for agricultural or hydroelectric purposes is almost axiomatic. A listing of the condemnatory evidence would fill several single-spaced pages. Let us use as representative case histories two of the biggest and most disastrous projects, the Volta project in Ghana and the Aswan scheme in Egypt.

Here is how the Ghanaian industrial-political complex trashed the Volta. Shortly after World War II a treasure in aluminum was discovered in the savanna of what was then a West African British colony, the Gold Coast. The great industrial groups proposed not only to mine the ore but also to construct the means to smelt it within the country. A few years later, when the Gold Coast gained independence and exercised the mandatory prerogative of liberation by changing its name, the president-for-life and self-styled "Saviour of the People," Kwame Nkrumah, seized upon the scheme as a means of propelling Ghana into an age of economic opulence and into political ascendency among the African nations.

The smelting of aluminum ore requires an enormous amount of electrical energy, and the potential for this high wattage lay hard by the ore deposits. The Volta River was to be dammed. Behind the dam would be created the largest artificial lake in the world. It was, at that time, the most ambitious engineering project ever proposed for tropical Africa.

The Volta has a vast watershed, extending to the west, north, and east of northern Ghana. The river enters Ghana as the Black Volta; after flowing some distance along the western border it is joined by tributaries to form the Volta, which courses, half a mile wide, through the equatorial forest. The river then emerges from Ghana's green mansions between two ranges of hills. Through a succession of turbulent rapids, the river descends two hundred feet within a few miles. Below the rapids, the river calms to flow through coastal plains, and finally it divides into a great deltaic system, before debouching into the Atlantic.

In 1966 the dam, two hundred feet high, was completed. Behind the barricade at the Adjena rapids a lake, ultimately 200 miles long, 8,500 square miles in area, with a 4,000-mile shoreline, began to form.

Before the lake was created, schistosomiasis was almost absent in the area. A survey in 1959 revealed that less than 0.3 percent of those living along the upper Volta and its tributaries were infected. The snail vectors along this stretch of river, *Bulinus globosus* and *B. (truncatus) rholfsi*, were not well adapted to rapidly flowing water. The consequently low numbers of snails would account in large part for the low level of infection. In contrast, the delta was like a huge aquarium filled with snails. *B. rholfsi* was abundant in the fresh-water lagoons, and in some delta communities 90 percent of the people were infected with *S. haematobium*.

With the filling of the lake a series of ecological changes occurred, producing a snail-schistosome chain reaction that triggered an infective explosion. The lake covered an area that had been savanna forest, with many hardwood trees. After inundation the trees died, and the dead trunks acted as a natural underwater palisade, braking wave action toward the shoreline. The resulting still waters were ideal for water weeds, and within a few years the inshore part of the lake was covered with a massive carpet of submerged weeds, predominantly *Ceratophyllum*. The vegetative growth was to provide food and shelter for the snails that were to make their way to the lake. The pioneer snail was *B. rholfsi*, which had lived in the small streams of the upper tributaries. As if sensing an abundance of food and shelter, snails of this species migrated to the lake, and within a short time changed in behavior from stream dwellers to lake dwellers. Now the snail population became massive. Enter the schistosome.

Fish colonized the lake, and fishermen colonized the lake shores. Farmers arrived to farm the lands about the lake. Villages and towns burgeoned, each settlement discharging copious amounts of solid waste (containing the schistosome eggs from infected fishermen). The organic matter encouraged further growth of aquatic weeds, which encouraged further growth of snails, which became infected by the miracidia hatched from the schistosome eggs. The infective cycle had been established.

As the lake filled to its final level the character of the shoreline changed. Where there had been only open beaches, many small coves and inlets began to form. Weeds (and snails) grew unmolested within these pockets of sheltered water. It was in these inlets that the fishermen beached their boats, and here they brought their catch on market days. Great crowds came each market day; villagers would wade into the water to buy fish and, unwittingly, to contract schistosomiasis.

But the children suffered most. The typically water-loving youngsters would come to the lake each day to play and bathe. Their contact with the water was intense. Daily, they were torpedoed by cercariae. By 1969 all—*all*—children between the ages of five and nine in many lakeside villages had *S. haematobium* in their pelvic veins. With puberty the telltale urine tinged with blood gave sign that they had come of age. Their bladders had been bartered for beer cans. And even that sacrifice was for almost nothing. The aluminum production failed to meet expectations, and Ghana's bright dreams of prosperity and political ascendancy faded.

On the other side of the continent another government, that of Egypt, was seeking to attain power and glory from a colossal water-impoundment scheme, the Aswan project. This project was bedeviled from its inception, first by politics—John Foster Dulles in pique denied American funding—and later by the havoc wreaked by ecological-epidemiological consequences. The Soviet Union came to the financial and technical rescue, and a dam 364 feet in height was built at Aswan, behind which the impounded water formed a lake 310 miles long, extending into the Sudan. The Nile was trapped and the river sickened, with bloating in the middle and dryness in the delta.

From its source in Lake Victoria, the Nile flows 3,500 miles to the sea. At Khartoum, in the Sudan, it is joined by the White Nile and this union enters the bleak Nubian Desert; then it flows into Egypt through the gorges and cataracts of Aswan, past the solemn ruins of Luxor and Karnak. It begins to widen as it courses through the fertile valley to Cairo. Below Cairo the great river disperses into a lacework of channels to create the delta that extends 150 miles from Port Said to

Alexandria. The Nile Valley and the delta have, since ancient times, formed one of the most populous and fertile areas of the world.

Into this cradle of civilization, the Nile—swollen by monsoon rains at its headwaters—has overflowed each autumn, bringing with unfailing generosity the rich organic silt that will nourish the next year's crops in the river valley and the deltaic basin. The early Egyptians, in homage to the river's fertile, life-giving force, depicted Hapi, the god of the Nile, as a physically feminized male—an amalgam of male strength and female bounty. The schistosome was present even in those ancient times. Mummies of the Twentieth Dynasty (1200–1075 B.C.) have been found to have mummified parasites within them. The pharaoh's daughter was undoubtedly at risk when she went to fetch the infant Moses from the waters of the Nile. However, until the building of the Aswan High Dam, the schistosome was largely confined to the delta; some 98 percent of the fellaheen there are infected, but as late as 1961 a survey revealed that no more than 5 percent of the population along the upper reaches of the river had schistosomiasis. The river's environment above the delta did not support a large population of snails, and at any rate the current was too swift to allow good contact between cercaria and human. Even in the endemic area of the delta there was an annual relief during the winter season, when the irrigation canals were allowed to dry out for about forty days and the silt, along with the snails, was dredged out.

In 1971, with the completion of the great dam at Aswan and the filling of Lake Nasser behind it, the epidemiology of schistosomiasis in Egypt changed radically. To begin with, the dam made continuous irrigation possible; the winter closing of the canals was no longer necessary. Year-round human activity and year-round fecal pollution intensified. This led to constant risk of superinfection and since the degree of pathological effect in a person depends in large part on the number of worms harbored, the people became yet worse stricken. In addition, the snail population now began to burgeon. The opaque, silted water of former times had tended to discourage the vegetation growth required by the snail. After the dam was completed the floods of yesteryear were no more and the waters ran clearer. Sunlight could now penetrate the water of the lower Nile, and that part of the river became colonized by masses of floating vegetation, cattails, and other reeds—a wonderful watery world for the snail. *Bulinus (truncatus) rholfsi*, the vector of *S. haematobium*, began to breed even more prolifically. What was even more disturbing, the population of *Biomphalaria alexandria*, the vector of *S. mansoni*, which was formerly present in only modest numbers, also began its explosive increase.

Finally, the upper Nile also became diseased. The water slowed. There was more vegetation and a consequent increase in the number of vector snails. Today, the prevalence of infection is still increasing in the growing communities along the Nile. In Lake Nasser an algal bloom has appeared, and snails, many of them already infected, are beginning to move into the area and establish themselves. It is only a matter of time before the lake becomes heavily schistosomatized.

The beneficiaries of the Aswan project were the snail and the schistosome; they flourish. Certainly the land was not a beneficiary; it lost its yearly rejuvenation of silt and became less fertile. Nor was the suffering sardine, which for reasons not completely understood all but disappeared from the Mediterranean waters near the mouth of the Nile after completion of the dam. The failure of the sardine fishery meant the loss of an important protein food source, and has brought poverty to thousands of fishermen. Nor were the fellaheen beneficiaries; they assumed an even greater parasite burden. But governments will have their dams, and as long as the chic of Araby have their way with the world's petroleum resources, hydroelectric power will be a seductive alternative, despite the capital costs for construction, staggeringly high to the energy-poor Third World. Unfortunately, the (hydro) electric bill too often contains a high schistosomal surcharge.

If schistosomiasis were present in Sweden or in the United States it would not be tolerated. The infected would be treated and hospitalized when necessary, with the costs taken care of through the national medical services (in Sweden) or through health insurance, Medicaid, or a second mortgage (in the United States). Lakes, rivers, ponds, and streams would be patrolled and warnings would be posted to the effect that "defecation in this water is a punishable offense." An army of scientists would be turned to the problem. No expense or effort would be spared in extirpating the worm from the citizenry. But schistosomiasis does not exist in affluent nations; it is an infection of the poorest people of the poorest nations. The peasant farmer and fisherman cannot afford Thomas Crapper's ingenious invention, the flush toilet, and will continue to relieve themselves in lake, river, and rice paddy. Present-day drugs are too expensive and noxious to be administered en masse by the usually inadequate and underfunded medical services. How then to loosen the schistosome's grip on its impoverished domain?

Prior to World War II the main emphasis in the control of vector-borne diseases, including schistosomiasis, was on personal and environmental sanitation; actions for this purpose ranged from sleeping under a mosquito net to draining swamps. Hygiene and sanitation were relatively effective but required constant attention and, often, large amounts of manpower and community participation. The postwar discovery of effective antimalarials and insecticides radically altered the strategy of control. If great masses of people could (theoretically) be protected by antimalarial drugs, why could they not be given schistosomicidal pills? If the anopheline-mosquito population could be reduced to an extent that interrupted transmission, why couldn't the snail population be similarly reduced by molluscicides? In the 1940s and 1950s a crossroads was reached in the development and selection of control measures, and the main road followed was paved with chemicals. The paths to control by biological means, environmental measures, or the development of methods to afford immune protection, diminished to relatively insignificant byways.

The synthetic promise offered by the antimalarials and insecticides was never fulfilled for the control of schistosomiasis. There is nothing comparable to the antimalaria pill that can be routinely taken at breakfast. I can bear personal witness to that. When I finally emerged from my nine-year sojourn in Africa, a routine medical examination revealed that I had acquired a light, asymptomatic infection of *S. mansoni*. At that time there was some evidence that Mansonian schistosomiasis caused or predisposed to liver cancer. The issue has been debated for many years without decisive resolution; there is a stronger case for the relationship of bladder cancer to urinary schistosomiasis. My friend and physician Alan Woodruff, professor of clinical tropical medicine at the London School of Hygiene and Tropical Medicine, is a cautious man, and with a "no nonsense from you, Desowitz," he had me admitted to the London Hospital for Tropical Diseases. He also assured me that he was in possession of a new sovereign remedy, a new form of antimonial compound that was free of the adverse side effects usual to antimonial drugs. The antimonials are organic preparations of the heavy metal antimony; they have been the sheet anchor for the treatment of schistosomiasis. But they have a medieval quality in that they kill the parasite just before they would do in the patient.

I entered the hospital hale and hearty to have a two week-course of drug infiltrated into the nether region of my person. The "nontoxic" drug produced an almost unbearably itchy rash and constant nausea, and made my heart's electrical circuitry do a few abnormal flip-flops. I had never felt so miserable. Since that time, drugs have been discovered that are somewhat freer of those side effects—but somewhat less effective. The point of my tale is that I had the closest and best medical attention, as well as the intellectual understanding to accept and perservere through the therapeutic course, while the average infected peasant, by contrast, would have none of these support systems. Probably, the severely affected persons of all economic and cultural strata would agree to treatment. However, if there is to be any impact on public health, all egg passers must be treated, and many of them are asymptomatic. Among those without symptoms, willingness to undergo treatment is very limited. At least one new drug, praziqantel, has shown efficacy and freedom from toxicity in its early trials. If this promise is confirmed, perhaps a satisfactory degree of control can be achieved, providing co-operation can be obtained from the untutored masses.

Except in limited demonstration trials, molluscicides have not proved to be any more effective than the drugs. Today's chemical snail killers have not been able to suppress vector populations over long periods of time or in large bodies of water. Except for the two-sexed vector of *S. japonicum,* all the snail vectors are her-maphroditic, so the few snails that survive molluscicide application can rapidly repopulate a body of water once the chemical pressure is removed. New, more potent molluscicides are in the works, as are baits to attract and concentrate the snails around the chemical depot. Undoubtedly some of these compounds will prove splendidly effective. They will also undoubtedly be stag-geringly high in cost, particularly those of petrochemi-cal derivation, and the invoice's bottom line will almost certainly deny science's bounty to those in greatest need of it.

Unlike most of the other afflicted nations, the Peo-ple's Republic of China decided, almost thirty years ago, to bite the bullet rather than await deliverance by research's promised missiles. According to the Maoist bestiary the threatening creatures—tigers, Americans (at a less amicable time), and schistosomes—have a dual nature. These enemies are at once formidably real and vulnerably weak. It was Mao's view that all of China's adversaries could be felled by the irresistible strength emanating from the collective will of the people. I think it a telling insight into the Chinese revolution that among the first targets to which this strategy was applied were the schistosome and the snail.

For many hundreds—probably thousands—of years, japonicum schistosomiasis had been one of China's most important health problems. In 1940 it was estimated that over 100 million people were at risk and at least 10 million infected. Whole villages were debilitated by hepatic schistosomiasis, and since these were mainly agricultural communities the economic loss to the entire country was serious. In 1949, within a year of taking power, the revolutionary government decided to launch an antischistosomiasis campaign, not only to improve health but also as a primary step in politicizing the populace by collective action. The Chinese realized that their industrial base was weak. They did not have the chemical industry to produce drugs and molluscicides in sufficient quantities for a national campaign. But they had people power; what they lacked in capital and technology was balanced by the labor potential from hundreds of millions of workers. In 1950 the "People's War against the Snail" opened with an intensive educational broadside. Peasants were informed about the disease and the strategy of the coming campaign by posters, radio talks, and lectures to village communes by the first barefoot doctors (the handbook given to these auxiliaries exhorted them to "be brave and not afraid of hard work"). During the next year hundreds of thousands of farmers, joined by teachers, students, soldiers, and factory workers, began the labor of dredging canals, draining ponds and swamps, building embankments, and even removing snails, one by one, with chopsticks. Snails of the genus *Oncomelania* (the vector of *S. japonicum*) were buried and suffocated beneath the dredged mud. Later in the campaign, molluscicides of local manufacture were applied to areas where the snails persisted. Mass fecal examinations were carried out and the individuals found infected were treated with the drugs that had been given priority of manufacture by the nascent pharmaceutical industry. But of paramount importance was the stern sanitation discipline imposed. Indiscriminate defecation was no longer permissible under the socialist way of life. A simple, odorless water-seal latrine was devised, in which worm eggs—not only of schistosomes but of all intestinal parasitic worms—were killed in the sedimented sludge. This simple sanitary device provided multiple benefits: it was a great success in reducing parasite transmission, the processed excreta were recycled as fertilizer, and the methane gas from the sedimentation tanks lit homes and cooking fires.

Although these measures have greatly reduced schistosomiasis in China, to a point where it is no longer a serious menace to health, the infection has still not been completely eliminated. The low levels of residual infection and snails are a slumbering threat. During the height of the antischistosomiasis campaign, Chairman Mao was moved to write the poem "Farewell to the God of Plague." The constant effort of community action keeps this malign god at bay in China, but in other parts of the world the health of millions continues to be sacrificed at his altar.

9

·

HARMONIOUS
PARASITES

Those of us engaged in teaching parasitology to medical students usually present a Grand Guignol pictorial display of the more devastating effects of our favorite pathogens. This show-business technique helps keep students awake in a course that might otherwise not rate too highly in the curriculum popularity polls. Even students who want to be psychiatrists (perhaps especially these students) rarely fail to respond empathetically to a photograph of the grotesque enlargement of the scrotum caused by filarial elephantiasis. The initial impression is that parasites are inevitably malevolent.

While the balance sheet would show that parasites undoubtedly do more harm than good, recent research has brought to light some curious and intriguing examples of parasitic infection that may contribute to the total health of the host. These are not merely oddments in the biological curiosity cabinet. The phenomenon of the harmonious parasite has greater import.

Modern medicine now appreciates—or rather, reappreciates, since the concept goes back to the ancient Greek founding fathers of medicine—that a causal relationship exists between the nature of our ailments and the character of the ecosystem in which we live. The unhappy affairs of the heart in industrialized countries are well known, as are the infectious diseases associated with primitive agriculture in the tropics. We tend to think of these societies and their ills as worlds apart, but the picture emerging from natural and experimental observations reveals a dynamic balance in which the diseases of one society can actually suppress those of another.

While the primitive and poor of the tropical world may lack automobiles, television sets, washing machines, and clothes dryers, they generally enjoy a freedom from hypertension and the cardiac problems suffered by the members of more civilized, affluent societies. Not only is abnormally high blood pressure conspicuously absent in these areas, but blood pressure does not rise with increasing age, as it does in Westernized, urban populations. Several explanations have been offered for this, such as diet and a mode of life without stress. Undoubtedly, these are important, but some investigators are not convinced that they are the complete story.

Studies conducted in a region of New Guinea where malaria is hyperendemic have concluded that this disease, as well as other chronic infectious diseases, causes a lowering of the blood pressure. In one investigation, the blood pressure of adults with enlarged spleens—a hallmark of malaria—was compared with that of individuals from the same village who had normal spleens. In those with the big spleens both systolic and diastolic pressure were lower than in the unaffected individuals. Similar results have been reported by a research team of the Papua New Guinea Institute of Human Biology, which studied two communities: one in the humid lowlands, where malaria transmission is intense; the other in the highlands, where lower temperatures inhibit the development of the malaria parasite in the mosquito vector. No one knows how malaria and other chronic infectious diseases lower blood pressure. With further research, scientists might be able to reproduce the effect without the infection, thereby alleviating the problem of hypertension in industrialized societies.

The heart attack, the civilized way of death, rarely occurs in the less sophisticated societies of the tropical world. High blood pressure and high blood cholesterol are the notorious factors implicated in coronaries. Again, the malaria parasite may be prophylactic, for it not only lowers blood pressure but also appears to decrease the cholesterol level.

Some years ago my colleagues and I carried out experiments to determine the long-term pathophysiological consequences of malaria in primates and rodents. One of the few consistent alterations in blood chemistry that we observed was a profound decrease in the amount of serum cholesterol in the infected animals. We did not obtain a precise understanding of the mechanism involved, but we hypothesized that the parasite either affected the cholesterol-processing tissues, notably the liver, or consumed the serum cholesterol for its own metabolic needs.

Still another possible beneficial result of infection by the malaria parasite arises from its influence on the immune response. So highly activated does the response become in attempting to mount a defense against the parasite that immunity to certain other antigens may be depressed. In some circumstances, to be sure, this is undoubtedly harmful. Children with malaria, for example, do not respond to inoculation for immunization against tetanus as well as do uninfected youngsters. Another example of how the effect of malaria on the immune response may be undesirable involves Burkitt's lymphoma—a form of cancer of the lymph system. Researchers have postulated that this cancer is caused by a virus that the immune system can usually suppress. The presence of the malaria parasite, however, may depress the surveillance of the immune system to such an extent as to allow the proliferation of the lymphoma virus.

On the credit side of the balance sheet, however, there is evidence that malaria prevents autoimmune diseases, such as lupus erythematosus, and inflammatory conditions, such as that scourge of the temperate zones, rheumatoid arthritis. Remarking on the rarity of these conditions in the endemic malaria zones, epidemiologists have pointed out the apparent importance of environmental factors rather than genetic predisposition. While the autoimmune and inflammatory diseases rarely occur in West Africans, American blacks of West African origin incur these conditions more frequently than do white Americans. Researchers have therefore directed their studies toward environmental factors, but they have not by any means fully explored the role of parasites.

To date, only a few experimental trials have tested the hypothesis that malaria suppresses autoimmune diseases. Two British scientists, B. M. Greenwood and A. Voller, have conducted one such investigation. They obtained a strain of mice that spontaneously developed autoimmune kidney disease and infected some of these animals with a rodent malaria, *Plasmodium berghei*. The uninfected control mice developed severe renal disease and died, while the malaria-infected animals (once the parasite infection had been resolved by self-cure) remained alive and well. The two researchers did not discover how the mice were protected from autoimmune renal disease, but suggested that the implications of their research might carry over to the treatment of such diseases in humans.

The beneficial effect of parasites on their victims is not limited to malarial infection. The lowly, ill-regarded intestinal worms may also do some good. The presence of these parasites may prevent certain pathological conditions of high prevalence in sanitized, worm-free populations.

One example of a situation of this type is provided by that vampire of the intestinal tract, the hookworm. Infection with hookworms causes an iron-deficiency anemia, but if the worms' toll is not too high and iron intake from food is adequate, the anemia is not so severe as to be markedly deleterious. Admittedly, chronic anemia cannot be advanced as a sign of blooming health, but even so, it may have a beneficial effect, another example of the exquisitely balanced give-and-take between infections. People with worm-induced iron-deficiency anemia are particularly resistant to bacterial infections. Only anemia of this type confers such protection. Patients with anemia arising from impaired function of the tissues that manufacture red blood cells or with hemolytic anemia (a condition in which red blood cells are destroyed—sickle-cell anemia, for example) appear to be fully susceptible to bacterial pathogens.

Some researchers have speculated that since many bacteria require iron as a metabolic element to sustain life, iron-deficient individuals do not easily support bacterial growth and proliferation. Another possibility is that a serum protein factor, transferrin, which may play an accessory role in the natural ability of serum to stop bacterial growth, is elevated in iron-deficient states. Although these studies require further confirmation and exploration, the results so far again suggest that a kernel of goodness exists within the seed of evil. And in the next chapter we shall see how, under certain conditions, the presence of intestinal helminth parasites may inhibit the development of asthma and other allergic conditions.

Virtually all living species shelter and nourish parasites. Indeed, even parasites may have parasites. Some parasites cause disease; others are inertly benign. Still others, such as those mentioned here, may actually provide some benefit. Natural and experimental observations on the effects of parasites in lower animals provide further evidence of the latter relationship. The primary measure of beneficence in these experiments has been the extent to which size and weight increase in the parasitized host.

One of the earliest observations on this phenomenon was made by that remarkable naturalist-parasitologist Miriam Rothschild. She found that certain estuarine snails parasitized by the developmental stages of a trematode (one of the class of flatworms that includes the schistosome blood flukes of man) were much larger than parasite-free snails. She reasoned that the increased size of the host, which involved soft tissue as well as the shell, is of great advantage to the parasite. Consequently, parasites with the faculty of producing this increase in size would have an evolutionary advantage.

Following Rothschild's lead, parasitologist Thomas Cheng and his colleagues at Lehigh University sought experimental confirmation of the enhanced growth in trematode-parasitized snails. Their studies revealed that the infected snails were heavier than the uninfected controls, but that this was due to a heavier shell rather than to growth of the soft parts. They attributed this effect to the parasites' destruction of the snails' digestive glands and the consequent release of calcium, which was then incorporated into the shells. Rothschild, however, believed that the parasite attacked the growth-regulating glands and in effect "caponized" the snails that she studied.

As we range about the evolutionary tree, we find other intriguing examples of parasites stimulating the growth of their hosts, provided they are not present in overwhelming numbers. Justus Mueller found that implantation of the larval stage of the tapeworm *Spirometra ranarum* into mice resulted in a weight gain that sometimes extended to obesity in his experimental animals. In this instance, it appears that, rather than altering the host's physiology, the parasite secretes a growth-stimulating, hormonelike substance.

Perhaps the most ardent champion of the harmonious parasite is David Lincicome, formerly of Howard University. He and his colleagues conducted a series of exemplary experiments in which they showed that rats and mice infected with *Trypanosoma lewisi, T. duttoni,* and the roundworm *Trichinella spiralis* (the cause of trichinosis in man) all grew significantly heavier than uninfected control rodents. What is even more amazing is that the trypanosome-infected animals lived considerably longer than their cohorts. In one typical experiment, the control mice lived an average of forty-nine days, while the animals infected with *duttoni* survived an average of eighty-two days. The apparent reason for the longevity is that the parasites provided the hosts with the essential energy-mediating vitamins thiamine, pantothenate, and pyridoxine.

Of course I do not counsel hypertensives, asthmatics, and those who desire to prolong the salad days of their youth to embark on a journey to the nearest malarial, parasite-infested pesthole. I do believe, however, that there is a lesson to be learned from a more tolerant view of host–parasite relationships. Too often, biomedical research takes a microcosmic, molecular approach, neglecting the clues so generously provided by the events of the natural world. This, I suggest, has been an important reason for our getting so relatively little bang for our research buck. By expanding our insights into these dynamic relationships and learning to control the effects without the infection, we may aid in reducing hypertension, asthma, and the velocity of aging.

10
THE WHEEZE
AND THE WORM

Every now and then those two Brahmins of the medical press, the *New England Journal of Medicine* and *Lancet,* play forum to a debate whose resolution affects the health of us all. Most of the arguments have been publicized in the popular press: Does a fat-free diet reduce the risk of cardiovascular disease? Do coronary-bypass operations benefit the patient more than the surgeon? Another question that has kindled a certain passion among a specialized coterie of followers of the papers and correspondence appearing in these journals and elsewhere has been, Can parasitic worms cause asthma? The ways of heart disease are well known to the laity, but the worm-asthma debate may be unfamiliar. However, to the two million American asthmatics, whose illness costs an average of 12 to 30 percent of the family income, any new revelation on the possible causes of this affliction is a breath of life.

If the association between asthma and intestinal worms seems peculiar, the origin of the story is even stranger. The opening chapter is set not in Nigeria or Nicaragua or some similar tropical country where the intestinal zoo is so common as to be taken for granted, but in Niagara Falls, Ontario. A doctor there, D. Tullis, noted that over the years there seemed to be an extraordinary number of asthmatic cases, 14 percent of all non-tuberculosis patients seeking medical attention at the Niagara Peninsula Sanatorium. He also found that the usual provocative agents, or allergens, such as pollen and the mites in house dust, did not seem to be the cause of asthma in the majority of these patients. With remarkable intuitiveness, considering Ontario's non-tropical location, Tullis decided to look for intestinal parasites in his patients. The search was indeed rewarding. After careful examination of fecal specimens, the sign of the worm—the characteristic eggs—was found in 198 of 201 patients with bronchial asthma, while all of the allergy-free controls were "clean." In 1971, Tullis published his findings in the *New England Journal of Medicine.* The worm-asthma hypothesis was quick to excite the interest of the biomedical community, and other studies were undertaken in an attempt to confirm Tullis's assertion. Confirmation was not forthcoming. In Boston and at the Mayo Clinic the investigators failed to find a single worm in any of their asthmatic patients.

The failure to confirm Tullis's findings didn't really eliminate the worm as a possible allergen. The argument continued, drawing fuel from the fact that while Boston, Massachusetts, is worm-free and Rochester, Minnesota, is worm-free, Niagara Falls, Ontario, because of its location, may not be. The Lake Erie bathing beaches are near the Welland Canal, which binds that lake to Lake Ontario. Through this canal there plies a lively international maritime commerce manned, in some cases, by tropical seamen, who carry as stowaways their intestinal parasites. The sewage discharge from these boats is thought to float to the beaches, where the infectious worm eggs are washed ashore. Under these unusual circumstances the local population is believed to be at risk to an ubiquitious triad of tropical parasites, the roundworm (*Ascaris lumbricoides*), the whipworm (*Trichuris trichiura*), and the hookworm (*Necator americanus* and *Ancylostoma duodenale*).

While this debate was taking place, a professor of pediatrics, Dr. Carolyn Coker Huntley, at North Carolina's Bowman Gray School of Medicine, proposed that the dog roundworm, *Toxocara canis*, was of equal, if not greater, importance in provoking asthma. *T. canis* is not sufficiently adapted to complete its development to sexual maturity in a human host. However, when the embryonated eggs, each containing a minute infective larva, are accidentally ingested, as they may be by a child grubbing about in contaminated soil, the larvae hatch; they are then fated to wander, strangers in a strange land, for years in the body tissues without maturing further. The infection, known as visceral larval migrans (VLM), is characterized by an enlarged liver, and serious lesions of the eye may result if the larvae invade that organ. Dr. Huntley observed that for many of her patients with VLM the initial presenting symptom was an asthmalike condition, and she suggested that there might be a considerable number of individuals in which VLM manifested itself mainly as a pulmonary disease. It was an intriguing surmise, but since it was based solely on clinical insights—for recovery of the microscopic larvae within the "haystack" of the body is almost impossible—it remained a theory without any experimental foundation.

The Huntley hypothesis was of particular interest to us in Hawaii, an island paradise that fulfills virtually all idyllic expectations except for a single flaw—it has the highest prevalance of asthma in the United States. Could some of the "Waikiki wheeze" be due to parasitic worms of the dog? Again we were confronted with the problem of making a direct, parasitological diagnosis, and giving asthma patients a provocative test dose of worm eggs was clearly unacceptable. However, parasites—whether worms, bacteria, or viruses—leave their distinctive spoor, the specific antibody the host produces in response to their intrusion. Using an exquisitely sensitive radioactive technique to measure specific allergy antibody (the class of immunoglobulin known as IgE), we tested the serum of asthmatic children to determine whether they had antibody specific for dog worms. We had some expectation that a few of the patients in our study would be serologically positive, but we were not just a little startled to find that 45 percent of the group had antibody to these parasites, while less than 10 percent of the nonasthmatic control group did. The immunological trail led not only to *T. canis* but also to the mosquito-borne parasite of dogs, *Dirofilaria immitis*.

D. immitis, better known to dog owners as heartworm, is an important cause of debilitating disease in canines. Only recently have we become aware of its potential threat to humans, it is now considered an "emerging zoonosis"—an infection transmissible from animals to humans. The life cycle of *D. immitis* is typical of filarial worms. Microfilariae, born of the female in the host's heart and pulmonary artery, circulate in the blood until picked up by mosquitoes, in which they mature into infective-stage larvae. The infected mosquitoes often bite humans and dogs indiscriminately, inoculating the infective larvae into either host. Like *T. canis, D. immitis* is incapable of completing its normal life cycle in a human; instead, it migrates to the lungs, where it produces a lesion that gives an X-ray picture very similar to that of a neoplastic malignancy. That is the extent, so far, of the clinical knowledge of human dirofilariasis, but like many other "new" diseases it undoubtedly has many other manifestations, perhaps including allergic hypersensitivity, that have not as yet been identified.

The worm-asthma hypothesis obviously provoked the interest of physicians and biomedical scientists working in the tropics. If the few Niagara Falls worms could cause so much asthma, the allergenic potential of the staggering worm burden of the warm regions would be enormous. If the theory was true, the globe's girdle between the Tropic of Cancer and the Tropic of Capricorn should be literally wracked by an enormous asthmatic spasm. Asthma had never been considered a significant medical problem in the tropics, but the multitude of diseases, many life-threatening, is so great there that "mere" allergy might have been overlooked by hard-pressed, overworked medical personnel.

Contrary to expectations, the epidemiological studies carried out in the tropics indicated that intestinal helminth parasites didn't cause asthma, but actually *prevented* it. Dr. R. C. Godfrey searched for asthma in Gambia, thet West African nation that extends, ribbonlike, on either side of the river from which it takes its name. He found that asthma was virtually absent in the rural population but common in city dwellers. The tillers of the soil harvest a personal crop of intestinal parasites, while the city's concrete, though it may make for mean streets, is relatively protective against these. Godfrey, basing his hypothesis on known immunological phenomena associated with helminths, attributed the absence of asthma in the country people to their plethora of worms. A group of workers in the Department of Medicine at Ahmadu Bello University, in Nigeria, came to essentially the same conclusion. Finally, there came an account from a self-parasitized parasitologist in England. In a letter to *Lancet,* Dr. J. A. Turton wrote that he had had severe hay fever each summer since the age of eight. Then, in the course of one of his experiments, he needed a regular supply of hookworm larvae and decided to become his own biological supply house. For two years he periodically infected himself with infective-stage hookworm larvae, and during those years he remained completely free from hay fever. Not once during that time did he have to resort to antihistamines for relief.

Finally, the pro-wormists and anti-wormists were joined by the no-wormists. Investigations carried out in Tanzania and Gaza failed to show any relationship between intestinal parasites and asthma. Asthma was found to be as prevalent among city dwellers as among farmers. There were as many asthmatics with worms as nonasthmatics with worms.

So now we have three propositions—one arguing that parasitic worms cause asthma, another arguing that parasitic worms prevent asthma, and a third maintaining that parasitic worms have nothing whatsoever to do with asthma. And the answer? Probably . . . yes . . . that is . . . under certain conditions and in certain individuals any one of the three relationships is possible. The logic to this confusion can best be understood if we examine the nature of allergy, of which asthma is only one manifestation.

Allergy is a kind of immune response, and in the

body's bureaucracy the immune system is the Immigration Service and the Defense Department. It screens and rejects foreigners and undesirables, be they parasites, microbial pathogens, neoplastic cells, or someone else's heart. The immune system is complex beyond belief and almost beyond understanding, but essentially it consists of two co-operating agencies; a cell-mediated, or cellular, arm and a humoral arm. The cell-mediated arm is staffed by macrophages that ingest and digest pathogens and other particulate matter and by cells that send chemical signals for the macrophages to assemble where needed. The humoral arm can be likened to a chemical-warfare branch whose cellular soldiers secrete proteins—antibodies (immunoglobulins)—when confronted by a pathogen or other antigenic substance. The antibodies produced in the reaction to a particular antigen have the specific configuration that allows them to combine with that antigen to zap it or otherwise render it innocuous.

So far so good. Without the development of an immune system, metazoan animals, including man, undoubtedly could not have evolved—or rather, survived to evolve—under the ubiquitous attack of the huge array of microbial enemies. However, the IgE allergy antibody acts somewhat differently from the others, and seems to make no adaptive sense. IgE does not combine directly with the antigen against which it was specifically elaborated, as do immunoglobulins of other classes. Instead, one end of the antibody molecule fixes to special receptor sites on the membranes of basophils (a type of white blood cell) and mast cells (a type of cell present in connective tissue). The basophils and mast cells are, in a sense, packets of potential biogenic dynamite. They manufacture and store histamine and other substances whose actions on blood vessels and other tissues are manifested by the symptoms of the allergic state. Fortunately, these biogenic substances normally remain safely within their cellular storehouses. They are released only when the cell-fixed IgE molecules are bridged at their exposed ends by the allergen.

That is the how of allergy. The why is still not completely understood, although we know that genetic predisposition and the nature of the provoking allergen both play a role. Five classes of immunoglobulins have been recognized—IgG, IgM, IgA, IgE, and IgD. When an individual is exposed to an antigen, certain specialized cells, the plasma cells, are switched on, begin to proliferate, and then turn to their business of manufacturing and secreting antibodies, of one of the five classes, that will specifically combine with the antigen. In most humans, IgM or IgG will be produced, but some individuals may switch on other classes. The controller at the switch is a pair of genes called the Ir genes. In allergic individuals the genetically directed response is, primarily, to trigger a proliferation of IgE-secreting plasma cells. Thus allergy is inherited, but only in the broad sense. For example, a person who is allergic to fish will not pass on that particular allergy to his or her children, but will pass on the tendency to become allergic. The allergen that plagues the parent may be very different from the one that plagues the child.

The chemical and structural immuno-acrobatics that make an antigen an allergen have not as yet been identified. It is known that certain antigens are more likely than others to switch on an IgE response. Pollens and the mites in house dust, for example, are more allergenic than bacteria and viruses. But of all the allergens, the parasitic worms are the most powerful in stimulating IgE production. In normal individuals the serum IgE concentration is less than 200 units per milliliter, in hypersensitives with pollen allergy it is some 400 to 600 units, while in people with worm infections it ranges from 1,000 to as high as 5,000 units. Some of this IgE is specific antibody for the worm, some of it seems to be nonspecific "rubbish" antibody, and some of it may be directed against completely different allergens, for it has been shown experimentally that worm infections can potentiate IgE antibody responses against completely unrelated allergens. If these observations are indeed correct, an individual with worms will be more sensitive to pollen, for example, than an individual without worms. To make matters even more confusing, other experiments have shown that some helminth infections suppress immune responses to unrelated antigens. In that case, our wormy person will be less sensitive to pollen than his "clean" counterpart.

Within this maze of conflicting experimental observations may lie the answers to the worm-versus-wheeze controversy. It is probably a matter of degree. The presence of a few worms in "immunological virgins," such as the patients in Niagara Falls, probably stimulates production of IgE antibody specific to the worms and/or potentiates elaboration of IgE specific to other allergens (right on, Dr. Tullis!). The presence of a large number of worms, and constant reinfection, such as occurs under the unsanitary conditions of much of the world's warm regions (if feces were fluorescent just about all of the tropics would glow at night) probably stimulates the production of nonspecific as well as specific IgE and thereby suppresses the immune responses to other antigens. The large amount of nonspecific "rubbish" antibody may have a "blocking" action; by occupying most of the mast-cell and basophil IgE receptor sites this antibody may prevent the release of histamine and inhibit allergic asthma (right on, Dr. Godfrey!). Worm loads of an intermediate magnitude may have no effect on the inhibition or production of asthma and the other declarations of allergy (right on, no-wormists!). Other factors, such as the kind of worms endemic to a particular region and the immuno-genetic character of the population, may also affect this speculative scenario.

Earlier I said that the immune response responsible for the allergic state makes no adaptive sense. What benefit can be gained from hay fever, food allergy, or asthma? But unless Darwin is to be denied, at some time in mammalian evolutionary development the allergic reaction must have been of some selective advantage—and it may have begun for the purpose of giving the intestinal worm an "asthmatic attack." All mammalian species have unwelcome worm tenants embedded in the mucosa lining their gut, and it has now been shown that IgE plays an important role in giving them an eviction notice. The IgE becomes fixed to the mast cells in the intestinal tissues, and when a parasite's antigens, probably its metabolic products, couple to the antibody, the cells near the worm release their packets of histamine and other pharmacologically active substances. These act on the parasite, giving it an "allergic spasm" that causes it to vacate its premises and be swept away in the fecal mass. Thus, when that first mutant plasma cell tentatively produced an antibody molecule that became fixed to host target cells, it may have been selected for perpetuation in man's distant ancestors because it was a kind of anthelminthic. Unfortunately, a good thing became a disaster; IgE-producing plasma cells eventually developed that recognized and responded to all the allergens that now bedevil us. Perhaps the secret of relief from allergy resides in the villain that could well have started it all—the worm.

11
•

DANGEROUS NYMPHS
OF NANTUCKET

The rich are not like you and me. They summer on
Nantucket and get babesiosis, hardly a household word
in the almanac of human ailments. Not readily recognized by the infectious-disease pundits or hotly pursued
by the parasitologist, the low-class *Babesia* parasite of
rodents has come to plague the residents of that idyllic
Massachusetts island.

Babesia parasites have long been known, particularly
for infecting domestic stock. In the warm, arid climate
of Australia, and at one time in Texas, babesiosis
resulted in enormous economic losses to the cattle
industry. And before the outbreaks on Nantucket, four
well-documented cases had occurred in humans, the
first of which was discovered in Yugoslavia in 1957. In
all of these cases, however, the infected individuals were
immunologically deficient. All of them had previously
undergone surgical removal of the spleen, an operation
that weakens one's immune system. Generally speaking,
however, these animal parasites were considered incapable of making the enormous leap to humans. But on

Nantucket in 1969 they crossed the barrier. The list of ecological-epidemiological ingredients that made this situation possible reads like the contents of a witch's caldron—sheep, deer, mice, ticks, *Babesia* parasites, bayberry, and scrubland.

From this brew emerged the evil genie that was to possess a long-time summer resident of Nantucket Island. The patient had enjoyed remarkably good health for most of her fifty-nine years, but in July 1969, she found herself in a New Brunswick, New Jersey, hospital. Two months earlier, she had closed her home in Santa Barbara, California, to make her annual summer pilgrimage to Nantucket, where she owned a pleasant estate in a scrubland area near the sea. Early in July, she began to suffer from a high fever, abdominal cramps, and a depressed state. A battery of medical tests failed to uncover the cause of her ailment. The fever persisted, the depressed state worsened, and the woman felt the will to live slipping from her.

A New Jersey physician vacationing on Nantucket persuaded the ill woman to enter the hospital he was affiliated with; there, in addition to her other symptoms, she was found to be suffering from pronounced anemia. Chance now intervened. A technician employed in the hospital laboratory, who had served in the Army Medical Corps in Vietnam, noticed forms in the patient's blood that were remarkably similar to the malaria parasites he had seen in Vietnam. The patient, however, had never traveled in the tropics and Nantucket is hardly an area of endemic malaria. The blood sample was then airmailed to the Center for Disease Control in Atlanta, where parasitologists provisionally identified the form seen by the technician as a species of *Babesia*.

The annals of medical literature are studded with

reports of infectious oddities—rare and often bizarre instances of alien pathogens infecting humans. Was this an example of one of these isolated cases, or did the woman's infection herald a true zoonosis—a disease communicable from animals to humans under natural conditions? The answer began to appear four years later, when a second person from Nantucket was diagnosed as having babesiosis. In 1975 seven more cases were reported from the island, and during the summer of 1976 another five vacationers were infected. At the time, a zoonotic outbreak of babesiosis seemed to have struck Nantucket; however, no new cases have been reported.

There are various species of *Babesia*, all composed of a wisp of cytoplasm and a minute dot of nucleus. Within the red blood cell of the host, the parasite appears deceptively similar to *Plasmodium falciparum*, the malignant organism that causes tertian malaria. Indeed, considerable parasitological connoisseurship is required to distinguish between the two. This morphological similarity has led to a diagnosis of malaria in some patients suffering from babesiosis.

Within the red blood cell the *Babesia* parasite divides asexually once or twice. The cell then disrupts, releasing the parasites, which proceed to invade other red blood cells. Not all the pathogenic mechanisms associated with babesiosis are fully understood, but anemia, due to continuing red-blood-cell destruction, is a hallmark of the untreated infection. Another symptom in humans is severe depression. Whether this is caused by a chemical reaction to the parasite is not known.

Unlike the malaria parasite, which has as its vector a mosquito, *Babesia* is transmitted by the tick, that grotesque arthropod that dog owners soundly curse each time their animals return from wandering in the underbrush. The *Babesia* reproduces within the tick, but this phase of biology is not well understood, mainly because its unisex appearance has made scientific spectatorship difficult. Researchers do know that the tiny wormlike offspring invade the tick's epithelial cells, undergo division, and finally invade the salivary glands. The parasite is then capable of infecting a warm-blooded host when the tick next feeds.

The gaps in our knowledge of *Babesia* biology illustrate the occasionally slow pace of scientific progress. In 1893, T. Smith and F. L. Kilbourne, two Americans studying cattle babesiosis in Texas (where it is commonly called red water fever) determined that the parasite was transmitted by the tick. The discovery that a parasite of warm-blooded animals could—indeed, must—jump the biological gulf to develop in an invertebrate in order to effect transmission boggled the scientific community.

Those who have suffered tick bites or attempted to dislodge a tick's mouthparts tenaciously buried in the skin will agree with Aristotle's complaint that ticks are "disgusting parasitic animals." They belong to the Arachnida, a class of arthropods that includes the spiders and mites. To survive, grow, and reproduce, ticks must drink the blood of their hosts. Most species partake of this sanguine diet by a kind of movable feast. After hatching from the egg, the small six-legged larva attaches itself to, and feeds on, a host; then it molts and becomes an eight-legged, sexually immature nymph (the term "nymph" must have been coined by an entomologist with a particularly mordant wit). The nymph continues feeding on the same host until adulthood; then it switches to a second, usually larger, host species.

Between meals, ticks of most species drop from their hosts and either hide on the ground or cling to vegetation and await a new host. In temperate regions, adults and immature stages of ticks can overwinter and then renew their search for a suitable host in the warmth of the late spring sun. Like virtually all other species of bloodsucking arthropods, each tick species possesses genetically programmed preferences and restrictions as to habitat and host. Whether a particular species can colonize a particular ecological niche depends to a great extent on its ability to withstand desiccation.

So much for the biology lesson. The diagnosis and subsequent escalation in the number of clinical cases of human babesiosis on Nantucket resulted in the mobilization of an army of experts. Scientists from the Center for Disease Control, the Harvard School of Public Health, and the Laboratory of Parasitic Diseases of the National Institutes of Health flocked to Nantucket to begin the detection work needed to determine the causative factors and the extent of the infection in humans and animals. The approach they took to understanding the *Babesia* outbreak is an example of how the exotic arts of the laboratory and the enigmatic arts of epidemiology can work in tandem.

Before the outbreak on Nantucket, babesiosis had never been considered a significant threat to public health, since only those who were immunologically compromised by loss of the spleen appeared to be susceptible. But the people on Nantucket who had come down with the disease had been healthy and normal prior to infection. That this circumstance did not fit the pattern of the European experience gave rise to the suspicion that a different, as yet unidentified, species of *Babesia* was involved in Nantucket.

Therefore, the first priority was to determine the species of the parasite. Fortunately for the investigators, the patients continued to show parasites in their blood despite chemotherapy and the abatement of their clinical symptoms. Blood from these patients was inoculated into a variety of laboratory animals. Three weeks after hamsters were inoculated in this manner, *Babesia* parasites appeared in their blood. A monkey also became infected. The species was identified as *Babesia microti,* a parasite commonly found in certain wild rodents throughout almost all of the temperate zone. What had happened? Was the Nantucket *B. microti* a mutant endowed with an ability to infect a broader range of hosts than its parent strain? Or had a peculiar assemblage of conditions brought man, tick, parasite, and rodent host together in such a way as to facilitate human infection?

An attempt was made to answer these questions by analyzing the *B. microti* species. Scientists compared the character of the enzymes from different *B. microti* isolates. The chemical processes that make life possible are catalyzed by proteins called enzymes, with a specific enzyme responsible for a specific step in the cell's chemistry. Since the basic chemistry of all life is remarkably similar, the same enzyme performs the same task (such as breaking down sugar for energy) in animals ranging from amoebae to zebras. But while they do the same thing, the enzymes of different species are not absolutely identical, and the differences in their physical properties can be revealed visually by the patterns the enzymes make when migrating in an electrified starch gel. The differences may be subtle, but the investigative method is so sensitive that it can detect mutation leading to incipient speciation.

Researchers employed this powerful probe—gel electrophoresis—to compare enzymes extracted from "Nantucket human" *B. microti* and from strains isolated from wild rodents inhabiting Nantucket and England. No differences were found.

While the parasite species had now been definitely identified as *B. microti*, the question of where it came from remained. Which species of rodents acted as reservoir hosts, and how prevalent was the infection among them? Using peanut butter as bait, the researchers trapped mice, voles, and rats. They discovered that only deer mice (*Peromyscus leucopus*) and voles (*Microtus pennsylvanicus*) were infected.

Now the *Babesia* species and the reservoir hosts were known, but researchers still had not identified the transmitting tick. The trapped voles and deer mice carried both larval and nymphal stages of two tick species. One was *Dermacentor variabilis*, whose adults feed mainly on dogs; the other was a species resembling *Ixodes scapularis*, whose adults prefer deer. The young of these species do not seek out rodents exclusively; they will bite humans who brush by the vegetation on which they rest. The species resembling *I. scapularis* has now been proven to be the vector.

The development of *I. scapularis* coincides neatly with the tourist season. In early summer the nymphal ticks, already infected with their charge of *Babesia*, await their next hosts. Although these are primarily rodents, humans will do. Most of the human babesiosis cases on Nantucket have occurred in late summer and early fall. The infections that occurred in the summer were presumably transmitted by the bites of nymphal *Ixodes* ticks. During the fall, the ticks feed on the blood of deer and then, as the weather turns colder, drop off to overwinter on the ground.

Finally, the investigators wanted to know the full extent of human babesiosis on Nantucket. Were the diagnosed cases only the tip of the iceberg, or did those with clinical manifestations represent the limit of the infection? Analyses of the data disclosed that all those with symptoms severe enough to seek medical help were older people, ranging in age from fifty-two to eighty-five. Most of them were economically well off. Generally, the more luxurious homes on Nantucket are located some distance from the sand dunes and beaches, in an area that, ecologically, is cheek by jowl with the scrub, the natural habitat of tick and deer.

Again, the laboratory served epidemiology. Infection, even when not clinically apparent, will elicit antibodies. These antibodies can serve as a highly useful telltale, their presence indicting who has or has had the infection. A full-scale "bleed" of Nantucket's permanent and summer population has not yet been carried out, but the results of the first "grab bag" sample suggest a moderate risk of infection. Approximately 2 percent of the people whose blood has been tested have shown antibodies against *B. microti*. Although a positive serological test is thought to indicate an infection acquired sometime during the past year, the great majority of these people have not recalled having any of the malarialike symptoms of the clinically afflicted. Apparently, in a mild case the symptoms may be so ephemeral as to go unnoticed.

While members of all age groups have evidently been infected, clinical babesiosis seems to be a senior citizen's disease. This finding agrees with the topsy-turvy immunological pattern that animal babesiosis has shown. Young domestic animals are highly tolerant of *Babesia* infection, while older animals are particularly susceptible. Ranchers have exploited this age-specific resistance by purposely infecting young stock; this procedure ultimately produces an immunity that protects them in later life. If older animals lacking the necessary antibodies were moved into tick-infested range, they would rapidly sicken with babesiosis and the mortality would be high.

We can only speculate about the historical dynamics that led to the present situation on Nantucket. Retrospective epidemiology is a difficult and sometimes dangerous exercise. And the problem of reconstructing the epidemiological events associated with Nantucket babesiosis is even more thorny because there is no precedent or parallel experience to guide the deductive process.

The visitor to Nantucket gets the impression of an area unspoiled and unchanged of permanence reaching to a distant past. The carefully nurtured and protected island is indeed a delight, but major changes in its landscape have occurred even within living memory.

Prior to colonial settlement, Nantucket was probably forested. Indians hunted deer here with the aid of selective burning, which seems to have caused little permanent ecological disturbance. During the mid-seventeenth century, British commercial enterprise began with the collecting of sassafras, which at the time was selling very nicely on the London market as an aphrodisiac. The early porn brokers were succeeded by a more somber lot of farmers, who made the island into a sort of ovine condominium, the land being held in common through a system of shares allotted to individual sheep farmers. The sheep population burgeoned and according to historical reports, reached an estimated 10,000 to 17,000 by 1855. Sheep are highly efficient grazers, and this large population not only deforested the island but reduced it to close-cropped pasturage.

Photographs taken in the early 1900s show grass unrelieved by a single tree.

Sometime during the nineteenth century the combination of dwindling forest cover and increased hunting eliminated the deer and probably the tick *I. scapularis*. The absence of tall vegetation produces a desiccating environment inimical to survival for many tick species. Indeed, for many years, the Russians have recommended intensive pasturage by domestic stock as a means of controlling ticks and tick-borne diseases.

In the mid-1850s, Nantucket's ecology again began to change as the island's economy slumped with the decline of both whaling and sheep raising. The common-land system had already come under attack by wealthy proprietors, who in 1812 had petitioned the Supreme Court to cede them large acreages. Later, cranberry farmers—and then the wealthy in search of summer retreats—progressively reduced the amount of land grazed by sheep. With the disappearance of the sheep, the island underwent a botanical transformation. Wes Tiffney, head of the University of Massachusetts field station on Nantucket, believes that the proliferation of indigenous bayberry facilitated the changes that took place in the former sheep pastures. He and his colleagues have shown that, like legumes, bayberry fixes nitrogen and thus enriches the soil. As a result, since 1890 most of inland Nantucket has grown up in heath and scrubland, ideal habitats for ticks. In 1830, settlers introduced pine trees to serve as windbreaks, and their spread into discrete forest stands provided the sanctuary necessary for the deer's comeback.

The first deer to return came by sea. In 1922, a Nantucket fisherman rescued an exhausted buck as it swam from the mainland. Four years later, two does were imported from Michigan, and additional deer were brought in during the 1930s. This meager nucleus has now produced a herd estimated at between five hundred and a thousand animals.

At some point during the reintroduction of the deer, the tick resembling *I. scapularis* covertly came with them. It, too, flourished, and it has now become the dominant tick species on the island. The reason for its proliferation is somewhat of a mystery. During entomological surveys of Nantucket in 1937, 1941, and 1944 no *I. scapularis* ticks were found. However, *I. muris*, a tick species exclusive to rodents, was abundant. This species probably cycled *B. microti* from rodent to rodent. By 1976 a striking change in the nature of the tick population had taken place. *I. muris* had virtually disappeared, and the *I. scapularis*-like tick predominated.

At this point, conjecture must embellish the facts. What brought about the change in the tick population? Was this change crucial for the transmission of *B. microti* to humans? The displacement of a native species by an introduced species has occurred many times in many ecosystems. Perhaps this occurred when the *I. scapularis*-like tick (henceforth referred to simply as *I. scapularis*) came to Nantucket. After all, there are just so many field mice to go around, and *I. scapularis* may have consistently come to dinner before *I. muris*. Then, too, the deer host of the *I. scapularis* adult is so much larger than the rodent host of the *I. muris* adult that it would be reasonable to assume that deer could support a much larger number of ticks. More adult *I. scapularis* ticks would produce more eggs and, in turn, more larvae, which could defeat *I. muris* in the competition for hosts.

If we make the broad assumption that human babesiosis did not occur in Nantucket prior to the establishment of a sizable *I. scapularis* population, we must ask why only this species, and not *I. muris,* transmitted the infection to humans. Perhaps *I. scapularis* is more catholic and aggressive in its tastes. The sheer density of *I. scapularis* may have also been an important factor. Another possibility is that this species occupied an ecological niche that gave it closer contact with humans than *I. muris* had. Or perhaps *I. scapularis* is a more efficient biological host of *B. microti* than is *I. muris.* Or a combination of some or all of these factors may be involved. Perhaps the true story will never be completely known, although the testing of these hypotheses in order to predict, prevent, or control babesiosis outbreaks in Nantucket and elsewhere would be important.

Nantucket should not be pictured as an island embattled by babesiosis. The clinical cases have, so far, been few and nonfatal. Nevertheless, the risk is there, and those who lack a spleen or are otherwise immunologically unresponsive should exercise caution if they visit the island. There is no drug to provide an easy cure. The antimalarials are ineffective, and the treatment given cattle is too toxic to be considered for humans except in a dire emergency. Nor is there a simple way to interrupt the chain of transmission, other than by reducing or eliminating the deer population. We do not even know the geographic limits of the infection. Isolated cases have occurred outside Nantucket—on Martha's Vineyard, Shelter Island, and Montauk, Long Island, but all the evidence now suggests that the conditions inherent on a tight little island are responsible for the continuation of the disease in humans.

Human babesiosis on Nantucket represents yet another assault on our sense of complacency. The truly great accomplishment of medical science during the last century has been the discovery of effective means to combat the infectious diseases caused by bacteria, viruses, and parasites. While vaccines, antibiotics, and the flush toilet have admirably protected us from many pathogens, the last war has not yet been fought. Old diseases like influenza and malaria are flourishing, and new ones like Lassa fever, legionnaires' disease, and human babesiosis are always a threat. If we accept the necessity of a strong military posture in times of peace, it seems just as reasonable to train and maintain an army of medical experts to combat these pathogenic invaders.

12

ITAMAE SAN, SASHIMI
NI MUSHI, GA IMASU!

(Waiter, there's a worm in my *sashimi!*)

Texts of medical parasitology are like counter cook-books describing the ethnic and cosmopolitan gastron-omic delights that serve as conveyances of infection. A steak tartare or hamburger rare may sow the seeds of beef tapeworm and toxoplasmosis. That ambrosial country sausage may produce a ten-foot-long pork tape-worm or, even worse, an acute, sometimes fatal case of trichinosis. The tourist to Asia who will "try anything once" may have a fluke (*Clonorchis*) implanted in his bil-iary tree or a Roto-Rooter-headed larva of the gnatho-stome burrowing through skin, soma, and brain after succumbing to the temptation of a dish containing raw fresh-water fish. And beware the drunken crab (uncooked fresh-water crab marinated in rice wine). That particular Asian specialty can deliver a worm (*Par-agonimus*) to lung and brain. It is no wonder that medi-cal students, a highly suggestible lot, are close to anorexia nervosa by the time they take their final examination in parasitology. For our students at the University of Hawaii school of medicine, particularly those of Japanese ancestry, only *sashimi* (raw marine fish) seems safe, and it is a sad day when I have to give the lecture on anisakiasis that will dislodge them from their last refuge of culinary comfort.

At night, lights from the small shops lining the narrow, serpentine side streets of Japanese cities beckon the passer-by. From within the restaurants, each displaying plastic pop-art models of the *spécialités de la maison,* issues a subdued conviviality of voices, with a promise of warmth. On an autumn evening, at the Season of the Chrysanthemum, a man whom we shall call Manabu Okada was making his way home through such a street after a trying day at the factory. As he passed a *sashimi* bar the thought of that fish nosh, complemented with warm saki, was irresistible. He entered through the curtained doorway and inspected the glass case on the counter which displayed slabs of raw fish and squid. Mr. Okada selected a rosy-pink piece of tuna, which the proprietor, with deft artistry, cut into thin slices. Each slice of the delicately flavored fish was dipped into a pungent sauce consisting of soy sauce, freshly grated horse-radish, and mustard powder. (A preparation of green horse-radish, *wasabi,* can be purchased at oriental food stores. I use Colman's mustard powder, adding enough mustard and horse-radish to the soy sauce to make my eyes water when I taste it.)

The inner man having been well served, Mr. Okada arrived home about 7 P.M., had a light meal, watched television for a short time, and was asleep by 9. He slept soundly until 3 A.M., when he was startled into sudden wakening by an abdominal pain so keen that it was like a *seppuku* sword piercing his stomach. Somewhat confused by the strangeness of the pain and the hour, he managed to stagger to the bathroom, where he agonizingly retched up blood tinged vomitus. Then he collapsed. His wife, thoroughly alarmed, called an ambulance, and Mr. Okada was rushed to a nearby hospital. The attending physician, after making certain Mr. Okada's condition was not life-threatening, began to ask questions, some of which seemed peculiar to the distressed patient. Had he eaten *sashimi* earlier that day? (Yes.) How long before the attack had he eaten *sashimi*? (About eight hours.) What kind was it? (Tuna.) How much did he eat? (One portion.) Satisfied that emergency surgery was not necessary, the doctor entered his provisional diagnosis of anisakiasis on the chart, requested a gastroenterological consultation, gave Mr. Okada a shot for his pain, and had him admitted to a medical ward.

In the late morning Mr. Okada, his pain somewhat blunted by drugs, was seen by a gastroenterologist. This specialist employed a fiber-optics gastroscope, a cunning instrument that enables the doctor to illuminate and inspect the stomach wall. The gastroscope's reconnoiter revealed the expected lesion, an ulcer approximately two inches in diameter located on the inner stomach wall. At the center of the ulcer's bloody crater a small, threadlike worm, its anterior end buried in the tissue, could be seen undulating leisurely. Still peering through the gastroscope, the doctor used a pair of remote-control pincers to pluck the worm neatly from the lesion. The laboratory parasitologist confirmed that the worm was an *Anisakis*-type larva. No one was surprised; several hundred cases similar to Mr. Okada's occur each year in Japan. Mr. Okada did not require surgical resection of his affected stomach, as some cases do, and within a few days felt well enough to be discharged, with a caution to stay off the *sashimi*. However, like most Japanese, he was gastronomically hooked on the fish and continued to indulge in the pleasures of the flesh.

While human anisakiasis remains a public-health problem in Japan, it has also been discovered, relatively recently, elsewhere. There is an international aspect to the trail of anisakiasis not unlike that of certain other parasites and the diseases they cause. For example, *Paragonimus westermani,* a trematode responsible for a serious lung disease in Asia, was first seen in a Bengal tiger that had expired in the Amsterdam zoo in 1887. Two years later Japanese doctors discovered the same parasite in the lungs of patients who had died of a pulmonary disease thought to be tuberculosis. The history of Mr. Okada's worm involved the same unlikely Dutch–Japanese connection. It began in 1955, when a fifty-one-year-old citizen of Rotterdam was suddenly seized by abdominal cramps so violent that he was rushed to a hospital, where emergency surgery was performed. When the surgeon exposed the abdominal cavity, the cause of the attack was revealed—an angry, bleeding ulcer, approximately two inches in diameter, in the ileal region of the small intestine. The offending lesion was excised, the wound closed, and the patient returned to the postoperative ward, where he made an uneventful recovery.

Only later, when the pathologist examined the preserved tissue specimen, was it discovered that this ulcer was far different from the "normal" gastrointestinal ulcers occurring in Holland. From the center of the inflamed, eroded tissue a 1½-inch worm protruded. Examination showed the worm to be a larval nematode of undetermined genus and species. At the time this was considered to be one of those isolated episodes in which a larval stage of an animal parasite makes an abnormal foray into human tissue, and the case was dismissed.

But over the next five years individuals with the same complaint of acute abdominal pain of sudden onset, and with no previous history of intestinal disease, began to appear in the emergency rooms of Dutch hospitals. Between 1956 and 1960 sixteen such cases were admitted to hospital. Eleven of them went to surgery, and in each of these, a larval worm was found in the swollen, hemhorragic intestinal wall. Clearly, a new disease had appeared on the Dutch medical scene. Several obvious questions had to be answered if the disease was to be understood and controlled. First, the nature of the parasite—its taxonomic status and its life cycle—had to be identified. Second, a determination had to be made as to whether it was truly an infection new to man, caused by one of those pathogens (such as *Babesia microti* and the Ebola-fever virus) that from time to time appear, as if suddenly and mysteriously spewed forth from an epidemiological maelstrom. Alternatively, it could be an infection that had occurred in Holland before 1955 but had gone unrecognized as to cause.

Identification of the worm proved to be more difficult than expected. In the immature stages the species of nematode parasites are not readily identified, because they lack the morphological landmarks of the adult that most parasitologists are familiar with. For this reason, or because the material didn't fall into the hands of the right expert, the parasite remained a taxonomic enigma until 1960. In that year some of the larval worms obtained from patients were examined by P. H. Van Thiel, a Dutch parasitologist familiar with the nematodes of both humans and marine animals. Van Thiel made the startling pronouncement that the larvae were *Anisakis*. The discovery was startling because *Anisakis* adults are parasites within the intestinal tract of marine mammals (porpoises and whales) and their larvae, during the course of the obligatory life cycle, are present in marine fish. The pieces of the epidemiological puzzle finally fell into place when another Dutch parasitologist, C. F. A. Bruijning, noted that the larval worms from humans with anisakiasis were identical to those parasitizing the herring caught in the North Sea.

The appropriate questions could now be asked of old and new patients with a confirmed diagnosis of anisakiasis. Had they eaten herring before their attack? If so, how had the herring been prepared? How long was the interval between eating the fish and the onset of abdominal pain? There was a unanimity of response that gave unmistakable evidence as to the source of the infection. All patients had eaten a lightly salted, uncooked herring locally known as green herring. Abdominal colic usually began about twenty-four hours after the meal, although in some cases the time interval was as short as four hours and in others as long as three days.

It was now assumed that this was a disease new to Holland, and the intriguing problem remained of what had caused its relatively sudden appearance. Though a new infection, such as anisakiasis, seems to arise from the void, there is always a reason for it—a new set of conditions that has brought the pathogen to humans. As far as can be determined, the two factors responsible for human anisakiasis in Holland were the introduction of a new way of preparing herring and a change in the traditional manner of processing the newly caught fish. Green herring was first placed on the market during the early 1950s. My Dutch friends tell me that their countrymen took to this raw, salted snack like Americans took to pizza. At about the same time that green herring was being introduced for public consumption, the traditional practice of eviscerating the fish while still at sea gave way to that of cleaning the fish ashore. The fish were iced after being caught, and often several days passed before they were brought to port and processed. In some fish, the larvae of the potentially pathogenic anisakid worms are naturally present in the flesh, but in herring, most of the anisakid larvae are normally located in the tissues of the intestinal tract, so the former custom of gutting the fresh herring immediately had rendered them fit for consumption even in the raw state. But now, as the iced fish cooled, some of the larvae were prodded into a migratory movement to seek the somewhat warmer protection of the musculature. Thus the green herring was now more likely to contain a worm.

When Japanese physicians read the Dutch publications, they realized that some of the patients they had seen over the years with similar symptoms could have had anisakiasis. Certainly, for sheer tonnage of raw fish consumed, no other people rival the Japanese. The first parasitological diagnosis of human anisakiasis in Japan was made in 1965. This was followed, within a few years, by almost five hundred more confirmed cases. Peculiar stomach lesions of unknown cause had been reported in the Japanese medical journals since 1940. Now that pathologists knew what to look for, they reexamined the tissue sections made from these patients' lesions, and this retrospective review brought to light several hundred more cases.

The recognition that nematode parasites of marine

animals could cause human disease stimulated a renewed effort to study the taxonomy, life cycles, host relationships, pathogenicity, and immunology of these worms. We are at mid-point in this research, and as at most research mid-points, there is considerably more confusion than at the beginning or the conclusion. There is, however, general agreement that all of the larvae recovered from the human cases are anisakine parasites. Anisakines are a large group of nematodes belonging to the same family as the ascarid of man, *Ascaris lumbricoides,* and the ascarid of canines, *Toxocara canis.* There are about twenty-four genera of anisakines; the exact number depends on whether the classification being used is that of a "lumper," a taxonomist who regards variants with minor morphological differences as belonging to a single species, or a "splitter," one who regards these minor morphological differences as indications of separate species. Adult anisakines are found in fish, reptiles, birds, and mammals, with different genera normally parasitizing different hosts.

The exact species of the larvae recovered from humans remains uncertain, and there is disagreement even on their genera. Working one's way through the taxonomy of these parasites is like being in a complex labyrinth whose exit has yet to be constructed. The Dutch cases, as well as most of the Japanese, seem to have been due to one or more species of *Anisakis,* the ascarid worm of porpoises and fish-eating whales. In addition, some of the larvae from cases in Japan and elsewhere have been identified as being a species of *Phocanema,* an anisakine parasite normally residing in seals. Experimental studies tend to confirm that only the larvae of "marine mammal" anisakines are capable of invading the tissues of an abnormal host, such as humans. When various kinds of larval anisakines were introduced into the stomachs of rats only those of "marine mammal" species were subsequently found to have penetrated the stomach wall.

The developmental cycles of all "marine mammal" anisakines appear to be similar. The adult female's eggs are shed, along with the host's feces, into the sea. The number of eggs produced daily is not known, but her "human" cousin, *Ascaris lumbricoides*, is a fecund marvel, laying 200,000 eggs each day of her life. The eggs sink to the sea floor, and within a few weeks a larva develops inside each one. When embryonation is completed, the larva emerges into the marine world. If the developmental journey is to continue, the larva must be eaten by the first intermediate host, a shrimp. The larva penetrates the shrimp's digestive tract and comes to lie in the body cavity, where it molts, grows, and awaits the next fateful event that will allow it to progress along the life cycle. This occurs when a fish or squid devours the infected shrimp. The larva bores through the stomach wall of the fish to become immured in the tissues. A few worms may penetrate to the viscera or musculature. In the fish the larva molts again, to become the infective stage. If a larger predatory fish eats the infected fish, the larva merely transfers to the new host. In this way the infective larva can be serially passed along the food chain a seemingly indefinite number of times—from squid to fish, or fish to squid, or fish to fish—without undergoing any further maturation. The final event in the cycle takes place when a marine mammal consumes the infected fish or squid. The larva escapes from the digested intermediate host and attaches itself to the stomach wall of the marine mammal, where it grows into a sexually mature adult.

Anisakid larvae have been found in fish from virtually all the world's briny waters—from tropical and arctic seas, from the Atlantic and the Pacific. A great variety of fish are parasitized, with the species of fish and the species of infecting worm depending on the nature of the fish and mammal population in the marine habitat in question. In coastal North Atlantic waters, where seals are relatively plentiful, pollack and cod are frequently infected with the "seal" worm, *Phocanema*. In the waters bordering Holland many herring are infected with the "porpoise" parasite, *Anisakis*. A recent outbreak of human anisakiasis in the Nantes region of France is believed to have been caused by the regional gastronomic specialty, raw sardines. All sorts of fish caught off both American coasts have been found to be infected—salmon, flounder, croaker, and mackerel, to name a few. When Dr. George Jackson and his colleagues at the Food and Drug Administration surveyed the fish sold in Washington, D.C. markets, they examined 1,010 fish belonging to twenty genera and twenty-three species and recovered 6,547 parasitic nematodes.

Those who dine on fish that has been baked, broiled, braised, or fried run no risk of contracting anisakiasis. Both cooking and freezing kill the parasite. The Dutch brought a rapid end to the outbreak of the infection by enacting legislation that required all herring to be frozen before being marketed. Such legislation is impossible in Japan. *Sashimi* cannot be prepared from frozen fish, and the Japanese would not forgo their deeply entrenched taste for raw fish in return for freedom from a disease that affects "only" several hundred people each year. At any rate, the variety of fish consumed as *sashimi* is too great for any legislation to be effective. In the United States, five cases of human anisakiasis have been documented, even though most Americans would, like my wife, classify raw fish as "funny food."

For some unknown reason, these North American cases have tended to be clinically much more benign than the infections experienced elsewhere. In fact, the first instance of American anisakiasis was discovered by chance, in 1972, when a seventy-six-year-old Massachusetts man required surgery to correct, by bypass graft, an aneurysm of the iliac artery (the blood vessel that runs along the small intestine). The diseased, atherosclerotic portion of artery was placed in a bottle of formalin after it had been removed, and nothing unusual was noted at the time. Later, when the tissue was about to be processed for histological sectioning, a three-inch-long worm was found in the bottle. The worm was subsequently identified as the larval stage of a species of *Phocanema*. How this man acquired the infection is somewhat of a mystery; he claimed that he ate fish infrequently and then only when it was well cooked. Nor did he have any abdominal complaints prior to surgery. Finding the worm was considered fortuitous, for there was no evidence that it had played any role in causing the aneurysm.

The other four American cases were even stranger in that the patients themselves coughed up and extracted the worms. A man in California who had eaten *sashimi* prepared from white sea bass purchased from a Marin County fish market felt a peculiar tingling sensation in the back of his throat ten days after this meal. He coughed, put his fingers in his mouth, and drew out a live, wriggling three-inch-long worm. A lady in Nova Scotia had a similar experience four hours after eating an undercooked cod fillet. So did an Ecuadorian lady living in New York, after preparing and eating *ceviche*, an Ecuadorian dish of marinated raw fish. All of these "throat" worms have been identified as the larval stage of the "seal" anisakine, *Phocanema*.

This variation in pathogenicity is perplexing. Do the different species of anisakine have different invasive potential, or is diversity among the human hosts involved? The only such diversity that has been suggested so far is in the amount of gastric juice, with the Japanese tending to have somewhat less than others. It is believed that the larval worms burrow better in less acidic conditions. Nor do we have, as yet, a full appreciation of the entire clinical orchestration of anisakiasis. Are there many asymptomatic infections like that of the man with the aneurysm, whose parasite was found only by chance? The answer to this problem will probably not be forthcoming until a specific serological test to detect these silent infections is perfected.

At the other end of the clinical spectrum, a study carried out by Sapporo Medical College's surgery department has some alarming implications, at least for Japan. This group studied the tissue sections, obtained during surgery, of patients diagnosed as having acute regional ileitis or Crohn's disease, whose cause(s) are currently unknown. After careful re-examination of this material, they concluded that at least half of the cases had been misdiagnosed. It was their opinion that the histological picture in these instances was more compatible with anisakiasis than with the intestinal disease originally identified. In fact, all or part of the worm was actually seen microscopically in the tissues of 140 out of 876 patients who had been diagnosed as having acute regional ileitis.

There is also much to be learned about the pathogenesis of what is considered to be typical intestinal and gastric anisakiasis. Since the human is an abnormal host, the larva that burrows into the wall of the digestive tract eventually dies without reaching sexual maturity. But while the intruder lives, it elicits an intensity of inflammatory response and a size of ulcerative lesion out of all proportion to its own relative minuteness. The esophagus of *Anisakis* has a large glandular portion, and secretions from it may be responsible for these untoward effects. But this is still speculative; secretions are yet to be isolated, characterized, and tested for pathogenic activity.

It would be some small comfort to be assured that humans have already acquired their full lot of parasites and other pathogens. At least there would be no surprises, and medical science could go about dealing with the old familiars. However, every so often a new germ or worm comes along to shake this complacency. And I must admit that the scientists present at the "birth" of a new human infection experience a special sense of excitement. As far as anisakiasis goes, those of us who like raw fish will continue eating our favorite preparations, worm or no worm. I had dinner last night at the home of a friend, a vivacious lady from the Cook Islands. She served Tahitian marinated fish—*poisson cru*—and I went back for seconds. It was delicious.

13

·

REGARDING *GIARDIA*

When all other diagnostic procedures fail to uncover the cause of a patient's intestinal discomfort and prolonged attacks of diarrhea, parasitological examination, the last laboratory resource of most American physicians, not infrequently reveals the protozoan pathogen *Giardia lamblia.* Most clinical laboratory parasitologists are reconciled to standing at the bottom of the diagnostic line. But when they find *Giardia* in a stool specimen they have an urge to editorialize in their laboratory report (I know, I do) with an "Aha! I told you so." Fortunately, in recent years, physicians have increasingly recognized *Giardia*'s widespread presence and pathogenic potential. This recognition is reflected in the editorial statement in the *Journal of the American Medical Association* that "giardiasis has assumed great importance recently in the United States because of increasing numbers of indigenously acquired and imported cases."

Giardia was first seen almost three hundred years ago by the man who fathered both microscopy and proto-

zoology, Anton van Leeuwenhoek. This wonderful
Dutchman had an all-consuming passion for the minuscule world he viewed under lenses, remarkably fine
for their time, that he himself had painstakingly
ground. His insatiable curiosity led him to search for the
presence of protozoa and other microorganisms—his
"animalcules"—in all sorts of material: rain water, pep-
per infusion, his own decayed tooth, shrimp heads, frog
feces. Nothing was too mean to escape examination.
Leeuwenhoek communicated his discoveries in letters,
hundreds of them during his long lifetime, to the Royal
Society of London. Each letter conveys a sense of excitement that has been similarly experienced by each suc-
cessive generation of microbiologists. Each time I turn
on the microscope lamp I still feel, as did Leeuwenhoek,
like a voyager embarking on a journey to a distant and
exotic land. There is, for example, childlike wonder in
his letter describing what he saw in frog feces. He
writes, "In the month of June I met with some frogs
whose excrement was full of innumerable company of
living creatures of different sorts and sizes. . . . The
whole excrement was so full of living things that it
seemed all to move." And so when he had a bout of
diarrhea in 1681 it was only natural for him to examine
a specimen of his own feces. In this way Anton van
Leeuwenhoek was the first to see the rapid movement
of the minute flagellate protozoan that 234 years later
was to be taxonomically baptized *Giardia lamblia.* At any
rate, Leeuwenhoek's discovery fell into the great sink-
hole of ignored observations until a certain Dr. Lambl
of Prague redescribed it in 1859 (calling it *Giardia intes-
tinalis*) and recognized its association with diarrheic illness.

But another hundred years were to pass, after

Lambl's report, before *G. lamblia* assumed its rightful place in the pantheon of parasites. When I was a student the argument still raged—or rather smoldered—as to whether it was pathogenic some of the time, all of the time, or none of the time. In the 1960s and 1970s the accumulated evidence, together with a series of spectacular outbreaks, finally brought recognition of its true pathogenic potential. The popular lay and medical press during the last decade carried a number of articles with such provocative headings as, "Serious Infection from Drinking Water Afflicts Visitors to the Soviet" (*New York Times,* March 10, 1974), "Giardiasis Endemic in U.S., May Be No. 1 Cause of Parasitic Diarrhea in Nation" (*Internal Medicine News,* January 15, 1974), and "Pennsylvania Investigates Illness that Beavers May Have Caused" (*New York Times,* November 4, 1979). There has also been a concurrent bloom of articles in the scientific literature reflecting the reawakened interest in the parasite and the infection on the part of clinicians, parasitologists, and immunologists.

Eventually the importance of *Giardia* as a pathogen would undoubtedly have been realized in any case, but the precipitating factor in bringing it to medical attention at this time had its origins in the improved relations between the United States and the Soviet Union. Soon after the Iron Curtain was raised, American tourists began to flood into the U.S.S.R.; by 1973 the Soviet embassy in Washington was issuing eighty thousand visas a year. During their stay, most visitors remain well except for occasional discomfort from a surfeit of *varnishkas* and vodka. Only after they return home do the unpleasant rumblings of giardiasis begin. Almost 25 percent of the travelers are stricken with the symptomatic troika—diarrhea, abdominal pains, and weight loss. The attack rate in some tour groups has been as high as 83 percent. The infection hasn't been confined to any particular species of traveler; it has found victims among students, touring teams of drum majorettes, agricultural experts, garden-variety travelers, and, with an insouciant disregard for high office, junketing congressmen. In addition, a significant number of infections have probably gone undiagnosed by home-town physicians and clinical laboratories unfamiliar with the parasite, for in the crowded medical-school curriculum parasitology has never competed for attention very successfully with pathology or sexology. Most American physicians are thoroughly experienced in identifying and treating diarrheas caused by enteric pathogenic bacteria that produce symptoms within hours or days after the contaminated food or water has been ingested. Giardiasis is more insidious, with an incubation period that usually lasts several weeks and the connection between the infective experience and the symptoms may not be recognized.

By 1973 the epidemiology of Soviet giardiasis had been pretty well worked out, thanks mainly to the sleuthing of Dr. Martin S. Wolfe of the State Department and Dr. Myron Schultz at the Center for Disease Control in Atlanta. Analysis of the places visited by tourists who had become ill showed that the majority of the infections were acquired in Leningrad. The plumbing of Tsar Peter's city had obviously fallen into disrepair. The tourist who drank water from the hotel room's tap or in a restaurant had no guarantee of its purity. At least some taps were dispensing fecally contaminated water. Only those tourists who drank tap water came down with giardiasis. The thirstier the traveler, the more tap water was drunk, the higher the risk of infection. The wise and wary who restricted their fluid intake to bottled water, beer, and wine were safe.

Although the Soviet Union has been singled out as a setting of high endemicity (not unfairly; Dr. Schultz in an editorial column of the *Journal of the American Medical Association* comments that Leningrad giardiasis is "unique in the annals of epidemiology"), the infection is actually a cosmopolitan found throughout the inhabited world. Except for pockets of high prevalence, an over-all infection rate of about 5 percent has been reported wherever stool surveys have been carried out, in both tropical and temperate regions. And it has been variously estimated that even in America, the land of gleaming bathrooms and the sanitized life, 2 to 20 percent of the citizens harbor *Giardia*.

The cause of all this intestinal distress is a minute protozoan which looks, when appropriately stained, like a clown. The racket-shaped motile form is a mere ten to twenty-five microns in length (a micron is a thousandth of a millimeter) and is equipped with eight flagella, two nuclei, and two slender rodlike structures that give it rigidity. On the under surface of the organism is an indentation, the "sucking disc," which allows *Giardia* to adhere to the cells of the small intestine's lining. When fresh specimens of frankly diarrheic stools or samples taken directly from the duodenum are examined under the microscope, the organisms can be seen moving in an indeterminate fashion, each one rotating about its long axis like the Red Baron doing wing overs in his Fokker. In the stained specimen the two side-by-side nuclei give the parasite the general appearance of a quizzical face peering back at the microscopist.

In the world beyond the bowel the motile form soon perishes, and it is the cystic stage, present in nondiarrheic stools, that is responsible for transmission from host to host. As the parasite travels down the intestine in the fecal mass it secretes a thin protective "shell" about itself to become a cyst. Within the cyst the dormant *Giardia* can remain viable for several months, given proper moisture. Sewage processing does not usually kill the cysts, and they will also remain alive (and infective) where chlorination of the water supply is inadequate. Contaminated water is the major source of infection, but salad greens (fertilized with feces) eaten in the tropics, mechanical carriage by flies from fecal filth to food, and carriage by hand from anus to mouth (not necessarily one's own) are also avenues of transmission.

There seems to be neither rhyme nor reason to cyst production. In some infected individuals large numbers of cysts are found in the feces at all times. In other individuals cyst production comes in waves, and for diagnosis of these cases it is necessary, to borrow the surfer's phrase, to catch a wave. In some cases only a very few cysts are ever shed, and these intermittently. In yet other cases cysts are never found in the stool specimen despite the presence of clinical symptoms (the degree and kind of clinical manifestations do not seem to be related to the presence or number of cysts). Understandably, those patients in whom cysts are produced sparsely and intermittently, or not at all, constitute a considerable diagnostic dilemma.

Nor is there convincing rhyme or reason for the wide spectrum of clinical manifestations of giardiasis, ranging from severe disease to apparently asymptomatic infections. The mechanisms responsible for this variable pathogenicity are little understood, and reports on them are conflicting. When I reviewed the literature, both old and recent, not long ago, I became more confused than ever. I also got a splitting headache. However, whatever the clinical manifestations and whatever the underlying mechanism of the infection, it can almost always be completely cured if the prescribed course of chemotherapy is followed.

In the most severe cases the ability of the small intestine to absorb fats, the sugar d-xylose, and in some patients vitamin B_{12} is greatly impaired. The fatty feces of these patients are foul-smelling and yellow-green. During the acute stage, which may persist from several weeks to several months, there is almost constant diarrhea, epigastric pain, nausea, flatulence, and loss of vim, vigor, appetite, and weight. The cause or causes of these intestinal abnormalities have not been elucidated. It has been suggested that by sheer numbers the parasites adhering to the upper intestine's lining constitute a physical barrier preventing absorption of fat and other substances. Two reports say that *Giardia* actually invades the epithelial cells of the intestine. Two other reports say it does not invade the epithelial cells of the intestine. A recent study has shown that in severe giardiasis with the malabsorption syndrome the intestinal cells are damaged and deficient in the digestive enzymes they normally secrete. Nor is it known why some individuals are so highly susceptible and others are not. Immunity undoubtedly plays a role, since visitors to an endemic focus are usually more affected than local residents. There is also accumulating evidence that those individuals who, because of their genetic constitution, fail to produce a normal amount of the immunoglobulin IgA are most severely affected. IgA is the "secretory" immunoglobulin, present in tears, saliva, and colostrum as well as being elaborated into the gut. IgA antibody is thought to play an important role in combating *Giardia* and other intestinal pathogens.

There have also been two interesting studies, one carried out in Melbourne, Australia, the other in Recife, Brazil, indicating that individuals with blood of group A are more likely to have severe manifestations than are other infected individuals. On the face of it, a relationship between blood group and susceptibility to giardiasis seems unlikely. But scientists are rarely at a loss for an explanation, and the hypothesis offered in this case is based on the fact that (for some unknown reason) a condition known as achlorhydria is most frequent in those with blood of group A. Achlorhydria is a physiological abnormality in which little acidic gastric juice is secreted and the stomach and adjacent small intestine are therefore much more alkaline than normal. The higher *p*H is thought to be favorable for the growth, and massive proliferation, of *Giardia*.

At the other end of the scale, a significant proportion of cyst passers (possibly as high as 50 percent of all those infected) appear to be asymptomatic. However, even people who do not complain may not be without complaints, and one long-term follow-up of cyst passers revealed that they had "stomach upsets" and loose stools much more frequently than members of the control uninfected group.

Somewhere in the middle of the clinical gradient is a group of diagnostic destitutes. Neither severely ill nor completely well, they are like a subculture of the distressed. These people have bouts of diarrhea often alternating with periods of constipation. Some have an almost constant sensation of queasiness. They have an underlying feeling of tiredness and are not infrequently depressed. The giardial origin of their illness is rarely recognized. The physician may not think of it. If giardiasis *is* considered, the single or multiple stool samples may be negative, or the parasite may not be detected by the inexperienced laboratory technician; no further examination of intestinal material is then undertaken. Finally, in desperation, many of these sufferers are sent to the psychiatrist for Freudian thaumaturgy to cure their "nervous bowel." These are the lucky ones. The less fortunate may end up in the hands of the surgeon.

My attorney was a typical example. Like most adults in this complex, disputatious world, I am hit from time to time by Fortune's slings and arrows and must seek legal counsel. My lawyer is a thoroughly nice man, but he lives over the hill—Oahu's Pali—on the other side of the island. I rarely see him between professional meetings. When I consulted him last, after an interval of five years, he looked dreadful. He had lost that feisty look, and that worried me. We like our legal gladiators to be aggressive in the judicial coliseum. After all, if they lose, *we* get fed to the lions. After I had unburdened myself of my anxieties, we got around to his troubles. He said that he had spent a good part of the past two years in the bathroom, heeding, as some authors on the subject put it, the "call to stool." The vague feeling of being unwell was so protracted and insidious that he fell into a state of asthenic anomie. The rounds had been made from physician to physician, from specialist to specialist. He received a lot of sympathy and a lot of bills but no help. One physician consulted was an infectious-disease specialist, but as my lawyer tells it, a stool sample was not examined until it was literally thrust upon that doctor. The single fecal specimen didn't reveal the causative organism. His description of the character of his feces—yellowish and rather greasy-looking—made his ailment sound suspiciously like giardiasis. I arranged to examine a series of his stools. Who can resist the sweet pleasure of counseling one's attorney? The first sample was negative; so were the second and third. But in the fourth sample, obtained about two weeks later, a few *Giardia* cysts were seen in a specimen that had been concentrated by special laboratory techniques. A chemotherapeutic course of metronidazole (Flagyl) was started the next day, and two months later, with an almost miraculous return to good health, he was off on a skiing vacation. I had also won my day in court.

My lawyer would probably not be amused by the knowledge that along with the customary health hazards of the sport, skiers have been at singularly high risk of contracting giardiasis—particularly in Colorado, where there have been two notable outbreaks, in Aspen and in Vail. By one of those strange quirks of fate, the 1964 Aspen outbreak was first signaled by a physician of the Center for Disease Control, who became ill after he returned from a ski holiday with 124 members of the Atlanta Ski Club. His inquiries turned up another four members with similar symptoms of diarrhea and intestinal cramps. *Giardia* was found in three of these four cases. The CDC physician alerted the Colorado State Department of Health, but by that time this agency had already received a dozen letters from irate skiers who had the post-Aspen downhill runs. Obtaining names from ski clubs whose members had vacationed in Aspen, the CDC sent a survey questionnaire to 1,350 people. Of the 1,094 who responded, 298 (27 percent) reported having had diarrhea some time after being in Aspen. The source of the infection was never pinpointed with absolute certainty, but circumstantial evidence incriminated the water supply. About half of

Aspen's water comes from a distant mountain creek and is distributed to three city wells. When a fluorescent dye was placed in the sewage system, a glow was subsequently detected in two of those wells. Clearly, the sewage was leaking into the water supply; moreover, *Giardia* cysts were found in samples from the sewage lines contaminating the wells. The city and its guests were fortunate that the epidemic was "only" of *Giardia;* the contaminated drinking water could just as easily have transmitted bacterial and viral pathogens.

Giardiasis hit Vail, the pleasure retreat of such notables as Gerald Ford, in 1978. Again, the epidemic was announced from a different part of the country, this time by a physician in Petoskey, Michigan, who treated a diarrheic family that had vacationed in Vail three weeks earlier. Epidemiologists, apparently sensitized by the Aspen experience, quickly mounted an investigation, which included a survey of 777 long-term residents of Vail. The findings weren't of much comfort to the health authorities (or, I suspect, to the Vail Chamber of Commerce); a full 60 percent of those surveyed reported having had a diarrheal illness sometime between January and April of that year. And once again it was raw sewage in the drinking water that was responsible. A blockage in a sewer line, discovered during the last week of March, had caused sewage to leak into the creek supplying water to the city. Cases continued to occur after the blockage was corrected because the contaminated water continued to be distributed, from storage tanks. As this water became diluted with fresh water the epidemic abated.

During the 1970s mini-epidemics of giardiasis flared in various parts of the nation—Kentucky, New Hampshire, Utah (affecting 34 of 52 students of a sociology

class who camped in the mountains and drank from a
stream), and Pennsylvania. But the largest and most
prolonged outbreak ever recorded in the United States
occurred in Rome, New York, where as many as 5,500
of a population of 50,000 are believed to have become
infected between November 1974 and June 1975. In
November, the Rome health authorities became concerned by the rising number of cases of gastroenteritis,
but there was no clue to the cause until January, when
Giardia was found in the stool specimens of eight
patients. By April, 1,200 stool samples had been examined. *Giardia* was the only organism commonly found in
these specimens; indeed, just three yielded isolates of
pathogenic bacteria. A house-to-house survey indicated
a symptomatic attack rate of 10 percent.

An epidemic of this dimension could be caused only
by a water supply contaminated with sewage. The route
of the city's water supply led from the watershed to a
reservoir to a creek to a treatment plant, where the
water was chlorinated, and finally to a pumping station,
from which it was distributed to the mains. When the
final product, the water coming from the tap, was
tested, the count of coliform bacteria (the standard measurement of water purity) was within acceptable limits.
Thus, unlike the Aspen and Vail outbreaks, this one
had not been caused by obvious contamination of the
water supply. But if by all conventional laboratory tests
the water was deemed to be potable, why was there so
much giardiasis? Part of the answer was provided by
Snoopy's relatives. Large amounts of raw water were
concentrated, and the sediment was fed to ten beagle
puppies. Twenty days later one of the experimental
dogs began passing *Giardia* cysts, and in two more weeks
so did another. The susceptibility of the dogs was con-

firmed when two other beagles came down with symptomatic giardiasis after being fed cysts of human origin. The investigators concluded that the Roman *Giardia* came from a human or animal source in the watershed area, and that the filtration and chlorination procedures that rendered the water bacteriologically safe did not kill the tough *Giardia* cysts. Other towns and cities with similar water-treatment practices can take scant comfort from this finding.

That dogs as well as humans were susceptible to infection also gave researchers something of a jolt. *Giardia* in dogs and cats had been described in the 1920s, but despite its morphological similarity to *G. lamblia* had always been considered a distinct species, incapable of cross-infecting humans. Now it seems probable that the species in the dog, at least, is the same as the human parasite. A few years ago another animal, the beaver, was also found to be a probable carrier of *G. lamblia*. The beaver hasn't had an easy time of it since the palefaces landed on these shores. It has been trapped in many areas to near extinction, and its habitats have been destroyed wholesale. Now it was accused of being a menace to human health. An outbreak of giardiasis in Bradford, a community in northwestern Pennsylvania, was thought to be due to infected beavers living in the streams above the town's water reservoir. The full zoonotic potential of dogs, beavers, and other mammals has not as yet been explored, although I suspect that not infrequently the human—for example, the careless camper defecating in a rural stream—may be more of a menace to the animal than the animal is to the human.

As every American tourist knows, the criterion of civilization is whether the faucet can be turned on and the water drunk with impunity. There are even some experienced travelers who would hold with the sentiment of the British of the more jingoistic era that the "natives" (and their water) begin at Calais. However, if the outbreaks of giardiasis and the undercurrent of chronic infection throughout our population are any indication, the pride we take in our pristine water supply may not be entirely justified. Alarms have already been sounded by public-health microbiologists that water-processing plants have fallen into disrepair and that in many cities and townships water and sewer lines are aging arteries. With tax coffers depleted and taxpayers groaning, meeting the costs of their repair or replacement becomes increasingly difficult. We are fortunate to have escaped so far with nothing more serious than giardiasis. To those infected, however, giardiasis is serious enough. And those whose infections remain undiagnosed and untreated are the walking wounded.

14

·

UNSEEMLY
BEHAVIOR

One of my favorite stories is about the stoned toilets of
Somalia. It seems that health advisers from a Western
nation were appalled by the toilet habits of the Somalis.
The entire country seemed to be covered with indiscriminately scattered human feces. Hardly a toilet, flush
or eny other kind, was to be found in this impoverished
nation. Fecally transmitted parasitic, bacterial, and viral
diseases were rife. So with all the best intentions, these
experts decided to use their government's aid funds for
a pilot project that would provide simple water-seal toilets to a selected village. In due course, several hundred
of the cast-concrete devices were placed over soak-away
pits that had been laboriously dug to the prescribed
dimensions. The advisers then returned to their offices
in the capital, satisfied that they had propelled these
people onto the road to modern sanitation.

A year later they returned to the village and were met
by a community elder, who courteously thanked them
for their gift. But he said, "They are, good sirs, useful

as seats, although not too comfortable. However, as toilets they are a mess." Somewhat surprised by this—what could go wrong with a water-seal toilet that had no moving parts?—they made an inspection tour of the latrines. The elder's description proved all too accurate. Each toilet was indeed a mess, clogged and rendered useless by a heap of stones and feces. The confused advisers questioned the elder. Why would anyone dump stones into a toilet? The elder looked surprised; everyone, he thought, knew that Somalis distracted themselves while defecating by clicking two stones together. And when they finished they dropped the stones into the most convenient receptacle—the water-seal toilet.

The tale of the toilets of Somalia provides a typical illustration of how behavior, unseemly and otherwise, perpetuates many diseases that drain the human resources of Third World peoples. Behavior is a crucial factor in the epidemiology of these infections, and in addition, the culturally rooted beliefs that influence behavioral patterns can be a formidable barrier to the application of available, potentially effective public-health remedies. Nevertheless, health professionals working in the tropical regions have largely ignored modification of behavior as a means of disease control. Nor have they taken into account the behavior and beliefs of the target populations when designing health campaigns. The notion persists among health authorities that high-technology panaceas can, by themselves, be effective. Many are surprised when their drugs, vaccines, and sanitation projects are rejected or allowed to fall into disuse. Educational persuasion has been the single concession to the need to induce behavioral change. But those of us who have evangelically displayed at village meetings charts showing the life cycles of parasites and the mechanisms of disease transmission know how futile this intellectualized approach to public health can be.

In developing this chapter's theme—the relationship of behavior to health—I should first like to return to the subject of bowel habits. My wife, a lady of intelligence and sensitivity, adamantly maintains that the reading public is not ready for a discourse on feces. It is with some temerity that I disagree. Shit as a source of infection with an array of pathogens is too important to be dismissed because of its aesthetic failings.

To a great extent behavior is an expression of physiological functioning. Therefore, a description of cultural idiosyncracies with respect to bowel habits should begin with the origin of the feces. For starters, there is the throw-away bit of trivia that the singular of *feces,* a plural word, is *fex*—pronounced "fakes." Feces are popularly regarded as the residue, the "metabolic ash," of nutritive intake. Actually, except for some cellulose bulk, they consist of water, intestinal secretions, and bacteria. The proteins, sugars, and fats of the digested food are absorbed in the small intestine, whereas water is absorbed in the large intestine. Diarrhea, the production of fluid or mushy stools, can arise from several causes: (1) conditions that speed up the passage of the food-fecal mass through the gut, thus preventing adequate water absorption; (2) functional failure of the large intestine to absorb water; or (3) abnormal exudation of fluid from the tissues into the intestinal lumen. Conversely, constipation, characterized by hard, dry, small stools, is due to slowed peristalsis, with correspondingly prolonged fecal passage. Abnormal fluid balance, as may occur with fever, can also cause constipation.

The normal American or European, whose diet has a relatively low fiber content, will pass a formed stool of about 100 to 250 grams within eight to seventy-two hours after eating—that is, about once a day. By contrast, the diet of the rural peoples of the tropics has a much greater cellulose content. This diet accelerates the transit of feces, and they tend to pass much bulkier stools two or three times a day. In addition, scholars of comparative bowel behavior have noted that these peoples are quick to heed the "call to stool." (When I come across this term in scientific papers it always evokes for me the image of a bugler blowing the refrain "Call to Stool.") One author who compared Westerners' behavioral ability to withhold defecation with that of the Africans in the group he had studied commented on the "phenomenal capacity of the young Bantu to defecate upon request." So it is unlikely that the rural peoples of the tropics would, or could, take time from their labors to visit a latrine, situated some distance away, several times a day—even if latrines were provided.

Nevertheless, one might think that with all of the great outdoors available, feces would be so widely scattered that contamination risks at any one point would be limited. However, the few studies carried out on defecation territoriality indicate that this is not the case. Humans, like most other social animals, seem to select very circumscribed areas in which to void their body wastes. An excellent model of this phenomenon has been provided by a group of parasitologists and anthropologists who examined the relationships of human behavioral factors to hookworm infection in a rural population in West Bengal. Their study is particularly fascinating in that it reveals how the behavior and biology of man and parasite interact with each other and with the environment both to perpetuate and to limit the infection.

After two years of interviewing the villagers and actually plotting the location of old and new fecal deposits, these investigators concluded that there were socially recognized defecation grounds, comprising in area only 1 to 2.5 percent of the settlement and its surrounding fields. The concentration of feces favored transmission. When passed to the ground with the feces, hookworm eggs embryonate rapidly and hatch. Within twenty-four hours an infective-stage larva has developed, which will live in the soil, awaiting the barefoot boy with cheeks of brown or his similarly unshod relative. At the first opportunity, the larva wiggles to the surface, penetrates the skin of the intruder, usually between the toes, and begins a migration through the host's body to the intestine. There it matures into a blood-sucking, anemia-inducing, adult. The larva does not spread very far from the fecal mass in which it has originated, so where the ground is heavily fecalized, as in Bengal, there is a potentially serious risk of infection.

Under these conditions a high rate of infection, accompanied by a high worm burden in each infected individual, would be expected. However, a parasitological stool survey of the population of the community showed that while a high percentage of the people were infected with hookworm, the average number of worms harbored was relatively low. A search was therefore made for behavioral factors which would account for this discrepancy, and indeed a delicate behavioral balancing act was found to be operating. On the regulatory side—limiting the extent of infection—was the fact that the Bengali was a quick defecator whereas the worm was a slow penetrator. The five minutes that the individual

spent on average in the defecating grounds was too
short to permit many larvae to find and enter the skin.
Religious custom also proved to be a limiting force. The
Hindu codex prescribes a set of rituals to offset what is
considered to be the polluting effect of defecation (one
Bengali religious text goes so far as to direct people to
face north in the morning while defecating and south in
the evening). The most important post-defecatory
imperative is ritual ablution, which is antiparasitic in
that it washes the adherent larvae from the skin.
Higher-caste Bengalis, who are more strict in this
observance, were found to have fewer hookworms than
members of the less orthodox lower castes.

The time when defecation habitually occurred also
affected transmission in various ways, both limiting and
enhancing it. Men were found to prefer to defecate in
the morning. The coolness and moisture during this
time of day made the larvae more active and viable—
and thus more infective. Men tended to have higher
worm burdens than women, who tended to defecate
more frequently in the afternoon. But the behavioral-
epidemiological interaction is even more complicated.
The larvae from the men's stools tended to die during
the heat of the ensuing day, while those from the
women's stools tended to survive and mature to the
infective state during the ensuing evening. For this reason the women were more of a menace to the men than
the men were to the women.

The greed of oil-producing nations and the resulting
deterioration in economic health of agriculturally based
tropical countries are contributing to the further spread
of fecally transmitted infections. The fertilizers produced by the petrochemical industry have, like all oil-
derived products, taken a mega-leap in price and are

becoming too costly for the native farmers, who are therefore returning to the ancient practice of organic farming—fertilization by feces. For the farmer, feces are becoming too valuable to discard. The feces of the fields multiply the foci of soil-transmitted infections, such as hookworm. The return to "night soil" as fertilizer contaminates the produce, producer, and consumer with a host of pathogens. For example, contaminated irrigation water becomes contaminated drinking and bathing water. The tropical countries can expect increasing threats to health with each incremental rise in the cost of crude oil.

Nothing frustrates, maddens, and depresses health workers quite so much as the public's indifference to, or rejection of, their carefully contrived projects. Things go better in affluent societies, where most of the citizens are aware of the causes of their diseases. Although the tropical poor are just as concerned about their health as the inhabitants of London or Los Angeles they haven't the foggiest notion of the germ or worm origins of disease, let alone the epidemiological intricacies responsible for the spread of these infections. Bad spirits, bad air, bad bananas, or a bad monkey that peed in the river are just a few of the agents considered responsible for illness. Given beliefs like these, it is no wonder that a Thai hill tribesman, for example, will make the government hospital or clinic his last port of call when ill. He will first seek medical attention from a local exorcist, who will prescribe herbs and perform a suitable ritual. If the illness persists, he will probably seek relief from another tribal medical specialist, who will attempt to blow the offending spirit out of his patient's ear. If this gives no relief, the tribesman will consult the third-echelon specialist, the injection doctor, a semiquack whose medical kit consists of a syringe, a hypodermic needle, and a supply of outdated antibiotics. Finally, *in extremis,* our tribesman will go to the government health assistant or physician. In American Samoa, where there is a fine medical service, I have seen children dying of bacterial diarrhea who, when finally brought to hospital, still had in their mouths the plant nostrums given to them by the *kahuna* (native priest-healer). The Samoan doctors helplessly complain that when these children die—as they too often do because by the time they are brought in it is too late for life-saving measures—the *kahuna* has the gall to admonish the parents, "See, you brought your child to the hospital and it died."

If beliefs, customs, ignorance, and apathy perpetuate disease and vitiate health services, what about the measures, useful in the control of some diseases, that entail no public participation? The application of insecticides to combat vector-borne diseases, such as malaria and onchocerciasis, and the construction of water and waste-treatment systems are two examples. Unfortunately, this type of strategy has not been notably successful in tropical regions. Vectors have become resistant to insecticides, and the capital outlay necessary to provide safe water to burgeoning populations has been more than most tropical countries can afford.

There is yet another approach to the control of infectious diseases—the mass administration of therapeutic agents, such as vaccines and drugs. This strategy incorporates both passive and active components. Government services supply and distribute the therapeutic agent (public passive), but the people must accept and swallow the pills or extend their arms for injection (public active). Generally speaking, national health workers have been efficient in organizing the logistics of these campaigns, but getting the drug to the people is only half the battle. Even where there is a satisfactory therapeutic agent, one that is safe, effective and cheap, the problem has been getting the people to the drug. Treating a sick individual patient is not difficult. The person under medical care is usually quite willing to take medicine. However, where mass administration of a drug is needed to break the links of disease transmission, cooperation is poor. There have been situations where a disease, such as malaria, could be almost totally controlled if the entire population could be maintained on the therapeutic or prophylactic course of the drug. During the first rounds of drug administration enthusiasm is great and 80 percent or more of the people accept treatment. Thereafter, participation rapidly wanes, until less than 10 percent are continuing the regimen, and the infection returns to precampaign levels.

I should like to tell you two cautionary tales about mass drug-administration campaigns. One campaign failed because its designers did not appreciate certain traditional aspects of the people's behavior and customs. The other campaign was successful because local customs and social structure were recognized and exploited.

THE CAMPAIGN THAT FAILED

A team of expert malariologists undertook to demonstrate how malaria could be controlled in northern Nigeria by the mass administration of chloroquine (an antimalarial drug). For their pilot project a village was selected in which malaria was highly endemic, and each week for a year the antimalarial pills were distributed to the inhabitants. At the end of the year the malariologists examined everyone's blood for the presence of malaria parasites, and were perplexed to find almost as much malaria as before the project began. Either the people were not taking the pills, or there were other complicating, unaccountable reasons for the lack of change.

The post-mortem analysis revealed that the failure was basically caused by customary and behavioral factors that conflicted with the project's design. It was found that many of the men, women, and children had not taken the antimalarial, and that the reason for this poor level of participation was different for each group. The men's rejection of the drug resulted from the failure to co-ordinate drug distribution with their food habits. The health workers went through the village giving out the pills at 7 A.M., before the men went to work in the fields. However, the men didn't eat their first meal until 9, and taking the pill on an empty stomach tended to induce nausea and vomiting. The children detested the bitter, naked pellet. For this group a chocolate-coated antimalarial should have been formulated. As for the women, it was impossible to determine the extent of their participation. The village was a Muslim community that enforced purdah. When the drug distributors passed the enclosed family compound, the women's hands appeared from behind the fence, as if disembodied, to receive the chloroquine. It remained uncertain how many of the village women actually received the pills, how many of those who received the pills swallowed them, and how many gave the pills to their children.

Even with the relatively low level of participation taken into account, the infection rate in both humans and vector mosquitoes still seemed inexplicably high. Again, analysis revealed that this high rate was due to certain traditional practices that the malariologists had been unaware of when the campaign began. The village had been selected because of its relative remoteness, which, it was thought, would isolate it from "contamination" by malaria carriers coming from untreated villages. But in fact there was a great deal of to-ing and fro-ing. "Controlled" villagers would walk miles to visit relatives or sell farm produce in distant untreated villages. And people from these untreated villages would come to the pilot-project village for the same purposes. This meant that new parasite carriers, sources of infection to the mosquito, were constantly being introduced.

What also puzzled the malariologists was the high frequency with which infants were infected. Here too, a probing into traditional practices provided the answer. Men from the pilot-project village often married women from other villages. When one of these women became pregnant it was traditional for her to return to her village of origin to give birth. The highly susceptible infant became infected in this untreated village and was a gametocyte carrier by the time it was brought home.

THE CAMPAIGN THAT SUCCEEDED

On the other hand there is Samoa and the campaign to liberate it from the grip of filariasis.

Mosquito-transmitted Bancroftian filariasis has been endemic throughout the islands of the Pacific basin since very early times. Captain Cook described the swellings of limbs that he saw when he visited Tonga. Herman Melville in *Omoo* gave an account of elephantiasis in Tahiti. Melville also noted that the Tahitians attributed the disease (this was in the 1840s) to the eating of

breadfruit and unripe yams. Change comes slowly to
the lovely high and low islands that bejewel the Pacific.
Surveys in the 1950s showed the infection rate in adults
to be over 50 percent in most of the inhabited islands of
Polynesia. In 1972, when we carried out a study in
Tonga using a new, highly sensitive diagnostic technique, we found that 45 percent of the children had
acquired filariasis by the age of two and virtually all of
the adults were infected.

Filariasis is unpredictable. Approximately half of
those infected remain essentially asymptomatic. The
others, the clinically affected half, suffer recurrent
fevers accompanied by painfully tender enlarged lymph
glands (the site of the adult worm). In a few of the
unfortunate, usually not more than 5 percent of those
infected, the disease irresolutely progresses to the grotesque enlargement of limbs and genitalia known as elephantiasis.

Nothing much could be done to treat the infection
until 1948, when the drug diethylcarbamazine (DEC,
produced under the name Hetrazan) was discovered.
DEC proved to be effective and safe; more than three
decades later it is still the drug of choice. Most important, it is so inexpensive that national health depart-
ments can afford to purchase the quantities required to
treat entire populations. The discovery of DEC thus
made it theoretically possible to control, and possibly
eradicate, filariasis in the relatively isolated islands of
the Pacific. To do so, however, would require total cov-
erage; the young and the old, the infected and the uninfected, those with symptoms and those without, all
would have to take the full course of the drug. This
might be readily feasible if the treatment involved just
one dose, but the most serious defect of DEC is that

multiple dosage over a period of weeks or months is required to eliminate the microfilaria infection. Also, the first dose produces transitory side effects—headache, fever, and joint pains—in some of the infected (but not necessarily symptomatic) individuals. Although subsequent doses do not give rise to these adverse reactions, word soon gets around, and everyone becomes drug-wary. For these reasons, most antifilariasis campaigns have been frustrated by widespread refusal to take the necessary doses of DEC.

The antifilariasis program in Samoa was not exempt from these problems. When health workers distributed the pills, the courteous people accepted them with a display of acquiescence and then either discarded them or took them home to be hidden away on a back shelf. A continuing high infection rate and a few discreet inquiries revealed what was taking place—or rather, not taking place. The government, still determined to carry out the program, enlisted the aid of the traditional communal leaders, the talking chiefs. Samoan society is in many ways feudal, and the talking chiefs continue to wield considerable power and influence over their villages. But in the end the talking chiefs provided more talk than action. While they did have influence over the people, theirs was a rule by consent and they did not dare exert the pressure necessary to force people to take the unpopular drug.

In desperation the organizers of the campaign finally consulted an anthropologist who was carrying out a study on the hierarchical power structure in a Samoan village. The advice of this behavioral scientist was to forget the health workers, forget the talking chiefs, and seek the aid of the women. It was his opinion that in their unobtrusive way the women held the stoutest staff of authority. And I assure you, Samoan women are very impressive—many are six feet tall and weigh over 250 pounds.

Somewhat doubtfully, the government acted on this advice. Health educators were sent from village to village to talk to the women, explaining the nature of filariasis and the strategy of the campaign. Once convinced, the village wives responded beyond all expectations. Perhaps many of them were influenced by the covert knowledge of the filaria-induced hydrocele, the swollen scrotum, hidden beneath the lava-lavas of their husbands. They banded together to form women's health committees. They planned treatment schedules and personally saw to it that every man, woman, and child took the full course of the drug, which they themselves distributed. No one escaped. A recalcitrant husband or son might flee to the hills to avoid treatment, but all his secret bolt-holes were known to the sorority and he was firmly marched back to the village to take his medicine.

Within two years of the first round of the women's war against filaria, the infection had virtually disappeared from Samoa. Unfortunately, for some unknown reason, in a few individuals DEC fails to clear all the microfilariae from the blood even after repeated therapeutic courses. These residual infections act as reservoirs and make it impossible to achieve total eradication. However, transmission was so reduced that for all practical purposes Samoa was relieved of filariasis for fifteen years. Now the prevalence rate is slowly beginning to rise again, and another antifilariasis campaign is about to begin. Happily, the women's health committees have remained intact in the intervening years. During that time they have continued their good work in other health areas, such as nutrition and immunization programs. It will now be a relatively simple matter to involve them in a new antifilariasis campaign.

The behavior causing the problems encountered by health workers in the malaria and filaria projects was "reasonable." For the most part it involved customs and patterns that could be understood by medical personnel. No profound imaginative leap is required for one to accept the fact that different societies will have different dietary habits, or that people of all groups will reject a therapy that produces adverse side effects, or even that some individuals in both affluent and primitive societies will seek medical aid from systems outside Western, scientific medicine. Given a modicum of intelligence and sympathy, we should be able to anticipate and deal with these problems. Occasionally, however, public-health professionals are confronted with a traditional practice or attitude so bizarre, so far removed from their intellectual frame of reference, that it brings their program to a numbing halt. This final story is about a personal experience of this kind of "alien" encounter. The experience was also one of the very few instances where research was potentially hazardous to my health—and life.

In 1961 my colleagues and I at the University of Singapore School of Medicine, where I was then employed, devised a serological method for measuring the antibody produced against malaria parasites. The test worked well in experimental mouse and monkey malarias and in the few cases of human malaria in the Singapore general hospital. However, to really prove its worth we wanted to evaluate the technique in a highly malarious community. The World Health Organization became interested and promised to find the necessary money if I would find the community.

Several days after WHO's letter promising support arrived, I had an unexpected visitor to my laboratory, Dr. Jan Saave, the medical officer in charge of the malaria-eradication program in what were then the Australian trust territories of Papua and New Guinea. Dr. Saave loomed in my laboratory door. He was a big man, not only in size but also in his florid imagination and in the intensity of his belief in his malaria program. He made me an offer I couldn't refuse. He would furnish the village for our study, an isolated Sepik community that hadn't as yet been subject to any malaria-control measures. He would join me in collecting serum specimens from the village's entire population in order to determine the level of antibody in the different age groups. After we completed this exercise, he would send in a team to begin mosquito-control operations by spraying with insecticide. Later, other malaria-program workers would trek to Salata (the village) to distribute antimalaria pills. In this way malaria was to be drastically reduced. We planned to return two years later to collect serum specimens again and determine if the people's immunity had been affected. It sounded ideal. Malaria was hyperendemic in Salata; there had been no previous control measures; and—I can now admit, after twenty years—best of all, it was in a wildly exotic setting I had always wanted to explore.

Some months after the meeting in Singapore, I arrived by air in Port Moresby. From there I flew in a satisfactorily large plane to Lae, where I boarded a very light aircraft that took me to a town called Maprik. Jan and jeep met me at Maprik, and we were on the road to Salata. Six kidney-jolting hours later the road dwindled to a path. It was now walking time. Porters had been sent ahead to meet us, and our entire group took off over hill and dale for the six-hour march to Salata.

I recall our arrival in the village as if it were yesterday. As we trudged up the final hill leading to Salata, Jan called out greetings in fluent pidgin. He then turned to me and said, "Bob, you are an important person, a professor; it is fitting that you be the first to meet the chief, so take your place at the head of the column." Flattered by this, I marched into the center of the village, where I met the chief in his full regalia of undress; a maquillage of many colors decorated his face, animal bones pierced nose and ears, and a pectoral made from a golden-lip oyster adorned his chest. I proffered my hand in friendship, and the chief extended his hand in reply. He then lowered his hand, grabbed my scrotum through my trousers, and gave a firm tug. I was about to howl in startled indignation when I heard Jan laughing uproariously. He was, of course, well aware of this traditional Sepik greeting.

With this testicular bond firmly established, our project went swimmingly. In the days that followed, hundreds of blood specimens were collected and hundreds of spleens were palpated for signs of malaria. Each morning Jan was busy treating the ailments of the Salatans. And Salata and its environs were exotic and beautiful beyond compare. Scattered through the village were several house tambarins, soaring cathedrallike structures of wood and thatch in which the men performed their most sacred rituals. On the outside, these Sepik temples were decorated with fancifully painted carved animals and mordant caricatures of human faces. Inside were large figures of gods and spirits, each endowed with a phallus of godlike size. In the filtered gloom of the house tambarin one could also find piles of human skulls, trophies of former battles (although some looked suspiciously fresh). At first light, the mist hovered over the jungle canopy surrounding Salata, and flights of sulphur-crested cockatoos gave raucous greeting to the new day. Some afternoons, a guide led me through the forest searching for sight of the breathtakingly beautiful birds of paradise. At night there were sing-sings, with dancing to the music of bamboo flutes. Each flute produced only a single note, and the melody was made by a consort of flautists in the manner of bell ringers ringing changes. We sat by the fire with the village elders, watching the festivities and sharing with them a bottle of transcultural wine. It was all very chummy, until the last day.

On the morning of our departure the spray team arrived and to demonstrate its efficiency immediately set to work. Within an hour Salata was under a cloud of DDT. This is when the trouble began. I heard a ululating cry from the crowd of "well-wishers" who had gathered to say good-by. Jan was in the center of an agitated group of men who were waving spears and stone axes about. Ah, I thought, our warrior friends have come to give us a ceremonial farewell. Unaware of any danger, I joined Jan in the warriors' circle to make a film record of these last moments in Salata. Jan, who had been talking very fast in pidgin, paused to whisper to me, "We're in trouble. Run for the path when I tell you." This seemed strange to me, but when I looked carefully and saw the enraged faces of our "friends," I became suitably alarmed. I also noticed the spray team cowering nearby. After a while Jan's explanations seemed to cool the hotter heads and a sort of amity was restored. Our porters collected the loads, and we began the walk to the road and the waiting transportation.

As soon as we were safely beyond the village, I asked Jan to explain what the incident was all about. I was astonished to hear that it was the yam that got us into the jam.

The yam is the basic food of the Salatans. It also plays an important role in the religious beliefs of these people. Huge ceremonial yams, some of them five feet long, are grown in sacred plots. Each is painted, and a superbly woven mask, to represent the spirit believed to inhabit the yam, is placed over one end. The yams are stored in sacred yam houses, and it was the spraying of these structures that caused the trouble. The Salatans had never seen DDT emulsion before and didn't know what to make of the white, milky fluid. They could think of only one similar substance—semen. The men of Salata decided that we were ejaculating, by way of the spray can, on their sacred yams. Why we would want to deposit semen on the yams they didn't know, but they did know that white men had some outrageously unseemly habits as well as peculiarly offensive medicines. They were convinced that spraying this "seminal fluid" was both a sacrilege and a means to defertilize the entire yam crop. They foresaw a year of starvation. Fortunately for us a few villagers had been to missionary school, and Jan was able to persuade them that the content of the spray cans was produced by the chemical industry, not by our prostate glands. They, in turn, (partially) convinced the other villagers. Still, an uncertainty lingered, and a compromise was reached; the sacred yam houses would not be sprayed. Also, rags were to be wrapped around the spray nozzles to prevent DDT from dripping onto any place where it might give offense to the spirits. As I recall the abject terror of the spray team, I very much doubt that any insecticide was applied after our departure. Certainly, malaria didn't decline in Salata until later, when mass chemotherapy was instituted.

To ameliorate, if not eradicate, the debilitating diseases of the tropics will require behavioral changes not only on the part of the populations at risk but also on the part of the public-health officials. Both the populace and the health worker must acquire a better understanding of the nature of the diseases and the preventive measures required. For the populace, doing this will mean surrendering many cherished beliefs and practices. For the health worker, trained in a scientific tradition quite different from that of the behavioral sciences, it will mean bridging a gap that has been described by the medical anthropologist Frederick Dunn as an "intellectual discontinuity . . . the long standing separation of the behavioral disciplines from the physical and biomedical sciences." Finally, for the researcher and those who fund research it will mean making the effort to raise their eyes from the microscope and take a new look at the world about them.

REFERENCES AND
SUGGESTED READING

CHAPTER 1

Cavalli-Sforza, L. L. 1972. Pygmies, an example of hunter-gatherers, and genetic consequences for man of domestication of plants and animals. In *4th International Congress of Human Genetics*, pp. 79–95. Amsterdam: Excerpta Medica.

Dasmann, R. F.; Milton, J. P.; and Freeman, P. H. 1973. *Ecological Principles for Economic Development*. New York: Wiley.

Desowitz, R. S. 1978. Health and epidemiology. In *Tropical forest ecosystems*. Paris: UNESCO.

———. 1980. Epidemiological-ecological interactions in the tropical savanna. In *Human ecology in savanna environments*, ed. D. Harris. London: Academic Press.

Dunn, F. L. 1968. Epidemiological factors: health and disease in hunter-gatherers. In *Man the hunter*, ed. I. De Vore. Chicago: Aldine.

Favar, M. T., and Milton, J. P. 1972. *The careless technology: ecology and international development*. Garden City, N.Y.: Natural History Press.

Lipton, M. 1977. *Why poor people stay poor: urban bias in world development*. Cambridge, Mass.: Harvard University Press.

Pavlovsky, Y. N. 1963. *Human diseases with natural foci*. Moscow: Foreign Languages Publishing House.

Vayda, A. 1969. An ecological approach in cultural anthropology. *Bucknell Review* 17:112–19.
Waddy, B. B. 1975. Research into the health problems of man-made lakes, with special reference to Africa. *Transactions of the Royal Society of Tropical Medicine and Hygiene* 69:39–50.

CHAPTER 2

Black, F. L. 1975. Infectious diseases in primitive societies. *Science* 187:515–18.
Fenner, F. 1970. The effects of changing social organization on the infectious diseases of man. In *The impact of civilisation on the biology of man.* ed. S. V. Boyden. Toronto, University of Toronto Press.
Weiner, J. S. 1980. Work and wellbeing in savanna environments: physiological considerations. In *Human ecology in savanna environments.* ed. D. Harris. London, Academic Press.

CHAPTER 3

Gajdusek, D. C. 1977. Urgent opportunistic observations: the changing, transient and disappearing phenomena of medical interest in disrupted human communities. In *Health and disease in tribal societies.* Ciba Foundation Symposium 49 (new series). Amsterdam: Elsevier-North Holland.
Subianto, D. B.; Tumada, L. R.; and Margono, S. S. 1978. Burns and epileptic fits associated with cysticercosis in mountain people of Irian Jaya. *Tropical and Geographical Medicine* 30:275–78.
World Health Organization, 1976. Research needs in taeniasis-cysticercosis. *Bulletin of the World Health Organization* 53:67–73.

CHAPTER 4

Bruce-Chwatt, L. J. 1977. Mathematical models in the epidemiology and control of malaria. *Tropical and Geographical Medicine* 28:1–8.
Cohn, E. J. 1972. Assessment of malaria eradication costs and benefits. *American Journal of Tropical Medicine and Hygiene* 21:663–67.

Conly, G. N. 1975. *The impact of malaria on economic development: a case study.* Pan American Health Organization, scientific publication no. 297. Washington, D.C.: Pan American Health Organization.

Elliott, R. 1972. The influence of vector behavior on malaria transmission. *American Journal of Tropical Medicine and Hygiene* 21:755–63.

Faust, E. C. 1939. Malaria mortality in the Southern United States for the year 1937. *American Journal of Tropical Medicine* 19:447–55.

Frederiksen, H. 1968. Elimination of malaria and mortality decline. In *Readings on population,* ed. D. M. Heer. Englewood Cliffs, N.J.: Prentice-Hall.

Garnham, P. C. C. 1966. *Malaria parasites and other Haemosporidia.* Oxford: Blackwell Scientific Publications.

Hall, T. F. 1974. The influence of plants on anopheline breeding. *American Journal of Tropical Medicine and Hygiene* 21:787–94.

Jeffery, G. M. 1976. Malaria control in the twentieth century. *American Journal of Tropical Medicine and Hygiene* 25:361–71.

Macdonald, G. 1956. Theory of the eradication of malaria. *Bulletin of the World Health Organization* 15:369–87.

Sinton, J. A. 1935. What malaria costs India, nationally, socially and economically. *Records of the Malaria Survey of India* 5:223–64.

———. 1946. Malaria in war. *Ulster Medical Journal,* May 1946, pp. 3–28.

Surtees, G. 1970. Effects of irrigation on mosquito populations and mosquito-borne disease in man, with particular reference to rice field extension. *International Journal of Environmental Studies* 1:35–42.

CHAPTER 5

Allison, A. C. 1954. Protection afforded by sickle-cell trait against subtertian malarial infection. *British Medical Journal* 1:290–94.

Boyo, A. E. 1972. Malariometric indices and hemoglobin type. *American Journal of Tropical Medicine and Hygiene* 21:863–67.

Edington, G. M., and Watson-Williams, E. J. 1965. Sickling, haemoglobin C, glucose-6-phosphate dehydrogenase deficiency and malaria in western Nigeria. In *Abnormal haeomglobins in Africa,* ed. J. H. P. Jonxis. Oxford: Blackwell Scientific Publications.

Luzzatto, L. 1974. Genetic factors in malaria. *Bulletin of the World Health Organization* 50:195–202.

Miller, L. H., and Carter, R. 1976. Innate resistance in malaria: a review. *Experimental Parasitology* 40:132–46.

Pasvol, G.; Weatherall, D. J.; and Wilson, R. J. M. 1977. Effects of foetal haemoglobin on susceptibility of red cells to *Plasmodium falciparum*. *Nature* 270:171–73.

———. 1979. Haemoglobin S and *P. falciparum* malaria. *Nature* 280:613–14.

Tobias, P. V. 1974. An anthropologist looks at malaria. *South African Medical Journal* 48:1124–27.

Wiesenfeld, S. L. 1967. Sickle-cell trait in human biological and cultural evolution. *Science* 157:1134–40.

CHAPTER 6

Desowitz, R. S. 1959. Studies on immunity and host-parasite relationships. I, The immune response of resistant and susceptible breeds of cattle to trypanosomal challenge. *Annals of Tropical Medicine and Parasitology* 53:293–313.

Duggan, A. J. 1962. The occurrence of human trypanosomiasis among the Rukuba tribe of northern Nigeria. *Journal of Tropical Medicine and Hygiene* 65:151–63.

Edge, P. G. 1938. The incidence and distribution of human trypanosomiasis in British tropical Africa. *Tropical Diseases Bulletin*, November 1938, pp. 3–18.

Ford, J. 1971. *The role of trypanosomiases in African ecology.* Oxford: Clarendon Press.

McKelvey, J. J., Jr. 1973. *Man against tsetse: struggle for Africa.* Ithaca, Cornell University Press.

Morris, K. R. S. 1960. Studies on the epidemiology of sleeping sickness in east Africa. III, The endemic area of Lakes Edward and George in Uganda. *Transactions of the Royal Society of Tropical Medicine and Hygiene* 54:212–24.

Mulligan, H. W. 1970. *The African trypanosomiases.* New York: Halsted Press.

Ormerod, W. E. 1976. Ecological effect of the control of African trypanosomiasis. *Science* 191:815–21.

Terry, R. J. 1976. Immunity to African trypanosomiasis. In *Immu-*

nology of parasitic infections. ed. S. Cohen and E. H. Sadun. Oxford: Blackwell Scientific Publications.

Vickerman, K. 1974. Antigenic variation in African trypanosomes. In *Parasites in the immunized host: mechanisms of survival.* Ciba Foundation Symposium 25 (new series). Amsterdam: Associated Scientific Publishers.

CHAPTER 7

Anderson, J.; Fuglsang, H.; Hamilton, P. J. S.; and Marshall, T. F. deE. 1974. Studies on onchocerciasis in the United Cameroon Republic. II, Comparison of onchocerciasis in rain-forest and sudan-savanna. *Transactions of the Royal Society of Tropical Medicine and Hygiene* 68:209–22.

Bradley, A. K. 1976. Effects of onchocerciasis on settlement in the middle Hawal valley, Nigeria. *Transactions of the Royal Society of Tropical Medicine and Hygiene* 70:225–29.

Choyce, D. P. 1972. Epidemiology and natural history of onchocerciasis. *Israel Journal of Medical Sciences* 8:1143–49.

Gunders, A. E., and Neumann, E. 1972. Parasitology and diagnosis of onchocerciasis. *Israel Journal of Medical Sciences* 8:1139–42.

Hoeppli, R., and Gunders, A. E. 1962. A comparison of skin changes caused by onchocerciasis and aging. *American Journal of Tropical Medicine and Hygiene* 11:234–37.

Hunter, J. M. 1976. *Geographical aspects of onchocerciasis control in northern Ghana.* World Health Organization document WHO/ONCHO/76.127.

Rolland, A. 1972. Onchocerciasis in the village of Saint Pierre: an unhappy experience of repopulation in an uncontrolled endemic area. *Transactions of the Royal Society of Tropical Medicine and Hygiene* 66:913–15.

World Health Organization. 1969. *Report of the joint US-AID/OCGE/WHO technical meeting on the feasibility of onchocerciasis control.* World Health Organization document WHO/ONCHO/69.75.

———. 1977. *Species complexes in insect vectors of disease.* World Health Organization document WHO/ONCHO/77.656.

CHAPTER 8

Bruijning, C. F. A. 1969. Bilharziasis in irrigation schemes in Ethiopia. *Tropical and Geographical Medicine* 21:280–92.

Dalton, P. R., and Pole, D. 1978. Water-contact patterns in relationship to *Schistosoma haematobium* infections. *Bulletin of the World Health Organization* 56:417–26.

Dazo, B. C., and Biles, J. E. 1972. *The schistosomiasis situation in the Lake Nasser area, the Arab Republic of Egypt.* World Health Organization document WHO/SCHISTO/72.23.

———. 1973. *Follow-up studies on the epidemiology of schistosomiasis in the Kainji Lake area, Nigeria.* World Health Organization document WHO/SCHISTO/73.29.

Eckholm, E. P. 1977. *The picture of health: environmental sources of disease.* New York: W. W. Norton & Company.

Faroq, M. 1964. Medical and economic importance of schistosomiasis. *Journal of Tropical Medicine* 67:105–12.

Jobin, W. R. 1980. Sugar and snails: the ecology of bilarziasis related to agriculture in Puerto Rico. *American Journal of Tropical Medicine and Hygiene* 29:86–94.

Klumpp, R. K., and Chu, K. Y. 1977. Ecological studies on *Bulinus rholfsi*, the intermediate host of *Schistosoma haematobium* in the Volta Lake. *Bulletin of the World Health Organization* 55:715–30.

Macdonald, G. 1955. Medical implications of the Volta River project. *Transactions of the Royal Society of Tropical Medicine and Hygiene* 49:13–27.

Malek, E. A. 1975. Effect of the Aswan High Dam on the prevalence of schistosomiasis in Egypt. *Tropical and Geographical Medicine* 27:359–64.

Negron-Aponte, H., and Jobin, W. R. 1979. Schistosomiasis control in Puerto Rico. Twenty-five years of operational experience. *American Journal of Tropical Medicine and Hygiene* 28:515–24.

Obeng, L. 1976. Goodbye to the god of plague. *New Internationalist,* June 1976.

Paperna, I. 1970. Study of an outbreak of schistosomiasis in the newly formed Volta Lake in Ghana. *Zeitschrift für Tropenmedizin und Parasitologie* 21:411–25.

Richards, C. S., and Merritt, J. W., Jr. 1972. Genetic factors in the susceptibility of juvenile *Biomphalaria glabrata* to *Schistosoma mansoni* infection. *American Journal of Tropical Medicine and Hygiene* 21:415–34.

Uhazy, L. S.; Tanaka, R. D.; and MacInnis, A. J. 1978. *Schistosoma mansoni:* identification of chemicals that attract or trap its snail vector, *Biomphalaria glabrata. Science* 201:924–26.

Van Der Schalie, H. 1974. Aswan dam revisited. *Environment* 16:18–26.

World Health Organization. 1967. *Measurement of the public health importance of bilharziasis.* World Health Organization technical report series 349.

———. 1976. *Water resources development and health. A selected bibliography.* World Health Organization document MPD/76.6.

Yokogawa, M. 1974. Epidemiology and control of schistosomiasis japonica. In *Parasitic diseases,* ed. M. Sasa. Tokyo: International Medical Foundation of Japan.

CHAPTER 9

Cheng, T. C. 1971. Enhanced growth as a manifestation of parasitism and shell deposition in parasitized mollusks. In *Aspects of the biology of symbiosis,* ed. T. C. Cheng. Baltimore: University Park Press.

Desowitz, R. S., and Langer, B. W. 1968. Hypocholesterolemia in rodent malaria (*Plasmodium berghei*). *Journal of Parasitology* 54:1006–9.

Elwood, P. C.; Mahler, R.; Sweetnam, P.; Moore, F.; and Welsby, E. 1970. Association between circulating hemoglobin level, serum cholesterol, and blood pressure. *Lancet* i:589–91.

Godfrey, R. C., and Gradige, C. F. 1975. Allergic sensitisation of human lung fragments prevented by saturation of IgE binding sites. *Nature* 259:484–86.

Greenwood, B. M.; Bradley-Moore, A. M.; Palit, A.; and Bryceson, A. D. M. 1972. Immunosuppression in children with malaria. *Lancet* i:169–72.

Greenwood, B. M., and Voller, A. 1970. Suppression of autoimmune disease in New Zealand mice associated with infection with malaria. *Clinical and Experimental Immunology* 7:805–15.

Hornabrook, R. W.; Crane, G. G.; and Stanhope, J. M. 1974. Karkar and Lufa: an epidemiological and health background to the human adaptability studies of the International Biological Programme. *Philosophical Transactions of the Royal Society of London.* B. 286:293–308.

Lincicome, D. R. 1971. The goodness of parasites. In *Aspects of the biology of symbiosis*, ed. T. C. Cheng. Baltimore: University Park Press.

Lincicome, D. R.; Rossan, R. N.; and Jones, W. C. 1963. Growth of rats infected with *Trypanosoma lewisi*. *Experimental Parasitology* 14:54–65.

Mueller, J. F., and Reed, P. 1968. Growth stimulation induced by infection with *Spirometra mansonoides* spargana in propylthiouracil-treated rats. *Journal of Parasitology* 54:51–54.

Salaman, M. H.; Wedderburn, N.; and Bruce-Chwatt, L. J. 1969. The immunodepressive effect of a murine Plasmodium and its interaction with murine oncogenic viruses. *Journal of General Microbiology* 59:383–91.

Weinberg, E. D. 1978. Iron and infection. *Microbiological Reviews* 42:45–66.

CHAPTER 10

Aderle, W. I. 1979. Bronchial asthma in Nigerian children. *Archives of Disease in Childhood* 54:448–53.

Carswell, F.; Meakins, R. H.; and Harland, P. S. G. 1976. Parasites and asthma in Tanzanian children. *Lancet* ii:706–7.

Chako, D. D. 1970. Intestinal parasites and asthma. *New England Journal of Medicine* 283:101.

Desowitz, R. S.; Rudoy, R.; and Barnwell, J. W. 1981. Antibodies to canine helminth parasites in asthmatic and non-asthmatic children. *International Archives of Allergy and Applied Immunology*, in press.

Godfrey, R. C. 1975. Asthma and IgE levels in rural and urban communities of the Gambia. *Clinical Allergy* 5:201–7.

Huntley, C. C. 1976. Of worms and asthma, or Tullis revisited. *New England Journal of Medicine* 294:1295.

Jarrett, E. E., and Kerr, J. W. 1973. Threadworms and IgE in allergic asthma. *Clinical Allergy* 3:203–7.

Joubert, J. R.; Van Schalwyk, D. J.; and Turner, K. J. 1980. *Ascaris lumbricoides* and the human immunogenic response. Enhanced IgE-mediated sensitivity to common inhaled antigens. *South African Medical Journal* 57:409–12.

Tullis, D. 1970. Bronchial asthma associated with intestinal parasites. *New England Journal of Medicine* 282:370–72.

Turton, J. A. 1976. IgE, parasites and allergy. *Lancet* ii:686.

Van Dellen, R. G. and Thompson, J. H., Jr. 1971. Absence of intestinal parasites in asthma. *New England Journal of Medicine* 285:146–48.

CHAPTER 11

Anderson, A. E.; Cassaday, P. B.; and Healy, G. R. 1974. Babesiosis in man. *American Journal of Clinical Pathology* 62:612–18.

Brocklesby, D. W.; Harness, E.; and Sellwood, S. 1971. The effect of age on the natural immunity of cattle to *Babesia divergens*. *Research in Veterinary Science* 12:15–17.

Healy, G. R. 1979. Babesia infections in man. *Hospital Practice*, June 1979, pp. 107–16.

Healy, G. R., and Ruebush, T. K. 1980. Morphology of *Babesia microti* in human blood smears. *Journal of Clinical Pathology* 73:107–9.

Healy, G. R.; Spielman, A.; and Gleason, N. 1976. Human babesiosis: reservoir of infection on Nantucket Island. *Science* 192:479–80.

Ristic, M; Conroy, J. D.; Siwe, S.; Healy, G. R.; Smith, A. R.; and Huxoll, D. L. 1971. *Babesia* species isolated from a woman with clinical babesiosis. *American Journal of Tropical Medicine and Hygiene* 20:14–22.

Ruebush, T. K.; Juranek, D. D.; Chisholm, E. S.; Snow, P. T.; Healy, G. R.; and Sulzer, A. J. 1977. Human babesiosis on Nantucket Island. Evidence for self-limited and subclinical infections. *New England Journal of Medicine* 295:825–27.

Spielman, A. 1976. Human babesiosis on Nantucket Island: transmission by nymphal *Ixodes* ticks. *American Journal of Tropical Medicine and Hygiene* 25:784–87.

CHAPTER 12

Chitwood, M. 1975. *Phocanema*-type larval nematode coughed up by a boy in California. *American Journal of Tropical Medicine and Hygiene* 24:710–11.

Hayasaka, H.; Ishikura, H.; and Takayama, T. 1971. Acute regional ileitis due to Anisakis larvae. *International Surgery* 55:8–14.

Jackson, G. J. 1975. The "new disease" status of human anisakiasis and North American cases: a review. *Journal of Milk and Food Technology* 38:769–73.

Jackson, G. J.; Bier, J. W.; Payne, W. L.; Gerding, T. A.; and Knollenberg, W. G. 1978. Nematodes in fresh market fish in the Washington, D.C., area. *Journal of Food Protection* 41:613–20.

Little, M. D., and Most, H. 1973. Anisakid larva from the throat of a woman in New York. *American Journal of Tropical Medicine and Hygiene* 22:609–12.

Myers, B. J. 1975. The nematodes that cause anisakiasis. *Journal of Milk and Food Technology* 38:774–82.

———. 1976. Research then and now on the Anisakidae nematodes. *Transactions of the American Microscopical Society* 95:137–42.

Petter, A. J. 1969. Enquête sur les nématodes des sardines pêchées dans la région nantaise. Rapport possible avec les granulomes eosinophile observés chez l'homme dans la région. *Annales de Parasitologie* 44:25–36.

Pinkus, G. S.; Coolidge, C.; and Little, M. D. 1975. Intestinal anisakiasis. First case report from North America. *American Journal of Medicine* 59:114–20.

Richman, R. H., and Lewicki, A. M. 1973. Right ileocolitis secondary to anisakiasis. *American Journal of Roentgenology, Radium Therapy, and Nuclear Medicine* 59:114–20.

Suzuki, H.; Ohnuma, H.; Karasawa, Y.; Ohbayashi, M.; Koyama, T.; Kumada, M.; and Yokogawa, M. 1972. *Terranova* (Nematoda: Anisakidae) infection in man. I, Clinical features of five cases of *Terranova* larva infection. *Japanese Journal of Parasitology* 21:252–56.

Van Thiel, P. H.; Kuipers, F. C.; and Roskam, R. T. 1960. A nematode parasitic to herring, causing acute abdominal syndromes in man. *Tropical and Geographical Medicine* 2:97–113.

Watt, I. A.; McLean, N. R.; Girdwood, R. W. A.; Kissen, L. H.; and Fyfe, A. H. B. 1979. Eosinophilic gastroenteritis associated with a larval anisakine nematode. *Lancet* ii:893–94.

Williams, H. H., and Jones, A. 1976. *Marine helminths and human health.* Commonwealth Institute of Helminthology miscellaneous publication no. 3.

CHAPTER 13

Brandborg, L. L.; Tankersley, C. B.; Gottlieb, S.; Barancik, M.; and Sartor, V. E. 1967. Histological demonstration of mucosal invasion by *Giardia lamblia* in man. *Gastroenterology* 52:143–50.

Brooks, S. E. H.; Audretsch, J.; Miller, C. G.; and Sparke, B. 1970.

Electron microscopy of *Giardia lamblia* in human jejunal biopsies. *Journal of Medical Microbiology* 3:196–99.

Giardiasis endemic in U.S., may be no. 1 cause of parasitic diarrhea in nation (article). 1974. *Internal Medicine News,* January 15, 1974, p. 32.

Gleason, N. N.; Horwitz, M. S.; Newton, L. H.; and Moore, G. T. 1970. A stool survey for enteric organisms in Aspen, Colorado. *American Journal of Tropical Medicine and Hygiene* 19:480–84.

Healy, G. R. 1978. The presence and absence of *Giardia lamblia* in studies on parasite prevalence in the U.S.A. In *Waterborne transmission of giardiasis.* Proceedings of a symposium, September 18–20, 1978, pp. 93–103.

Moore, G. T.; Cross, M. W.; McGuire, D.; Mollohan, C. S.; Gleason, N. N.; Healy, G. R.; and Newton, L. H. 1969. Epidemic giardiasis at a ski resort. *New England Journal of Medicine* 281:402–7.

Morecki, R., and Parker, J. G. 1967. Ultrastructural studies of the human *Giardia lamblia* and subadjacent jejunal mucosa in a subject with steatorrhea. *Gastroenterology* 52:151–64.

Pennsylvania investigates illness that beavers may have caused [article]. 1979. *New York Times,* November 4, 1979.

Raizman, R. E. 1976. Giardiasis: an overview for the clinician. *American Journal of Digestive Diseases* 21:1070–74.

Schultz, Myron. 1975. Giardiasis [editorial]. *Journal of the American Medical Association* 233:1383–84.

Serious infection from drinking water afflicts visitors to Soviet [article]. 1974. *New York Times,* March 10, 1974.

Shaw, P. K.; Brodsky, R. E.; Lyman, D. O.; Wood, B. T.; Hilber, C. P.; Healy, G. R.; Macleod, K. I. E.; Stahl, W.; and Schults, M. G. 1977. A communitywide outbreak of giardiasis with evidence of transmission by a municipal water supply. *Annals of Internal Medicine* 87:426–32.

Wright, S. G.; Tomkins, A. M.; and Ridley, D. S. 1977. Giardiasis: clinical and therapeutic aspects. *Gut* 18:343–50.

CHAPTER 14

Belcher, D. W.; Neumann, A. K.; Wurapa, F. K.; and Lourie, I. M. 1976. Comparison of morbidity interviews with a health examination survey in rural Africa. *American Journal of Tropical Medicine and Hygiene* 25:751–58.

Dhillon, H. S., and Kar, S. B. 1963. *Investigation of cultural patterns and beliefs amongst tribal populations in Orissa (India) with regard to malaria eradication activities.* World Health Organization document WHO/MAL/384.

Dunn, F. L. 1979. Behavioural aspects of the control of parsitic diseases. *Bulletin of the World Health Organization* 57:499–512.

Ekwueme, O. 1978. Bowel habits in Ugandan villagers. *Tropical and Geographical Medicine* 30:247–51.

Gillett, J. D. 1975. Mosquito-borne disease: a strategy for the future. *Scientific Progress* 62:395–414.

Gratz, N. G. 1974. *Urbanization and filariasis.* World Health Organization document WHO/FIL/74.119.

Hoeppli, R. 1957. Early Tahitian views on elephantiasis. *Zeitschrift für Tropenmedizin und Parasitologie* 8:41–48.

Kochar, V. K.; Schad, G. A.; Chowdhury, A. B.; Dean, C. G.; and Nawilinski, T. 1976. Human factors in the regulation of parasitic infections: cultural ecology of hookworm populations in rural West Bengal. In *Medical anthropology,* ed. F. X. Grollig and H. B. Haley. Chicago: Aldine Publishing Company.

Najera, J. A.; Shidrawi, G. R.; Storey, J.; and Lietaert, P. E. A. 1973. *Mass drug administration and DDT-indoor spraying as antimalarial measures in the northern savanna of Nigeria.* World Health Organization document WHO/MAL/73.817.

Penaia, L. 1971. *Annual report 1971, filariasis control project.* Apia: Government of Western Samoa.

Reuben, R., and Panicker, K. N. 1978. A study on human behaviour influencing man-mosquito contact, and of mosquito biting activity on children in a south Indian village community. *Indian Journal of Medical Research* 70:723–32.

INDEX

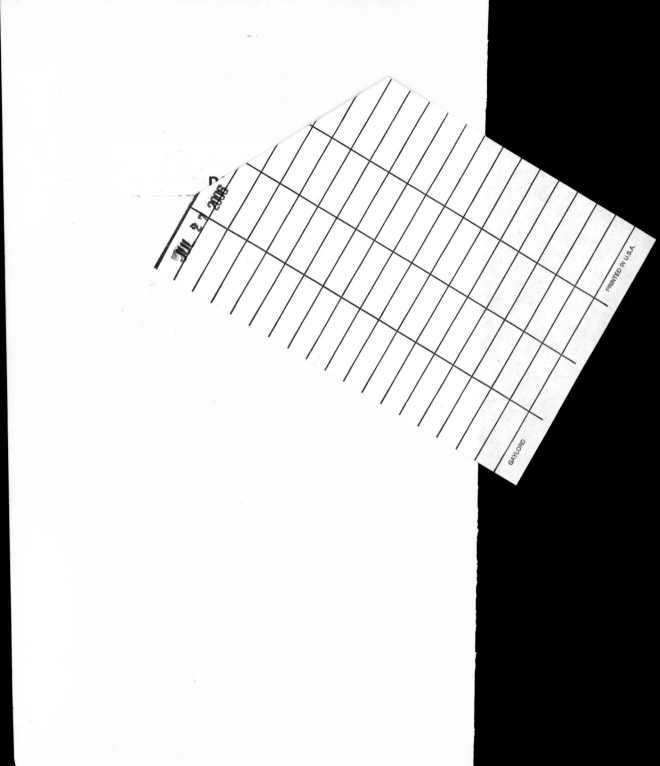